MIND_Movers_
Creative Homework Assignments Grades 3–6

MIND*Movers*
Creative Homework Assignments Grades 3–6

Diane Hart

Margaret Rechif

Addison-Wesley Publishing Company
Menlo Park, California • Reading, Massachusetts
Wokingham, Berkshire, U.K. • Amsterdam • Don Mills, Ontario • Sydney

This book is published by the Addison-Wesley Innovative Division.

Design: Irene Imfeld
Illustrations: Jane McCreary

The blackline masters in this publication are designed to be used with appropriate duplicating equipment to reproduce copies for classroom use. Addison-Wesley Publishing Company grants permission to classroom teachers to reproduce these masters.

Copyright © 1986 by Addison-Wesley Publishing Company, Inc.
All rights reserved. Printed in the United States of America.
Published simultaneously in Canada.

ISBN-0-201-20090-2
DEFGHIKKL-AL-96543210

CONTENTS

Introduction   1

Unit 1: Getting Acquainted   5
    All About Me   7
    This Is My Life   15

Unit 2: Homework Habits   23
    Homework—When?   25
    Homework—Where?   33

Unit 3: Spelling   41
    Learning to Learn Spelling Words   43
    Detecting Spelling Patterns   51

Unit 4: Time Well Spent   57
    How Long Does It Take?   59
    Television Time   67

Unit 5: Mastering Multiplication   73
    Seeing Double   77
    The Fives Facts   83
    The No-Sweat Nines   87
    The Perfect Squares   90
    The Last Facts   94

Unit 6: Communities   99
    Plant and Animal Communities   101
    Grandparents' Communities   111
    A Parent's Community   121
    My Own Community   129
    Bike Town—Planning a Community   139

Unit 7: Business Ventures   143
    Goods and Services   145
    Testing the Market I   151
    Testing the Market II   157
    Business Costs and Setting a Price   163
    Open for Business   173
    My Business Career   181

Unit 8: **Holidays** 187
Halloween Treats 189
Thanksgiving Turkey Talk 199
A Special Gift 207
Martin Luther King Memorial Speech 215
Community Valentines 223
Arbor Day Tree Study 231
Planning a Festival, Celebration, or Fiesta 241

Unit 9: **Study Aids** 259
Homework Schedule 261
Cluster Diagram 262
Paragraph Planning 263
Individualized Spelling Sheets 264
Spelling Patterns 267
Making a Presentation 269
Writing a Letter 272

Introduction

MindMovers contains one year's worth of weekly homework assignments, ready to be used as is. As you and your students go through these assignments you will discover that:

- Each assignment is presented in a clear, concise, easy-to-follow manner with expectations for students spelled out clearly.

- The assignments are appropriate for students at grades 3 to 6 in any school setting. The homework topics can easily be integrated into standard curriculum areas such as reading, writing, math, and social studies.

- The assignments help students establish good homework habits and time-management skills. They also introduce students to useful tools for organizing, memorizing, and communicating information.

- Most of the activities in the assignments involve higher-level thinking skills.

- Each assignment comes with suggestions for classroom integration and extensions for Gifted and Talented Education (GATE) students. The assignments can also be used as the basis of an in-class or pull-out GATE program.

- Home/school communication improves when you make use of the sample letters to parents at the beginning of each unit.

- Parents enjoy the fact that many assignments involve them in appropriate and helpful ways.

- Students enjoy doing these assignments because they are varied, interesting, and based on everyday life.

- The process of giving and receiving back homework assignments changes from a chore to an adventure for both you and your students.

Weekly Homework Folders

You and your students will be better organized if you make simple homework folders for children to take home on Mondays and return on Fridays. A pocket folder can be made with two 12-by-18-inch sheets of construction paper and a stapler.

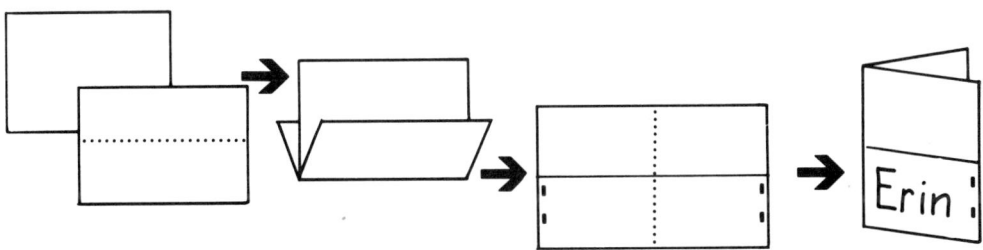

Fold the first sheet lengthwise and drop the second sheet into the fold. Staple the ends to form pockets and then fold the sheets crosswise like a book. Write each child's name on the front of a homework folder.

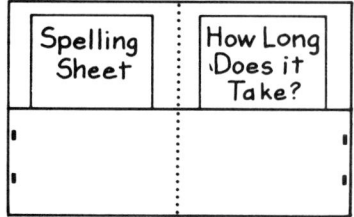

Each week staple a new homework schedule to the front of the folder (see Unit 9). It may get lost if you don't attach it firmly.

At the same time, tuck each student's Mind Movers assignment and any other homework sheets into the inside pockets of the folder.

Before long your students will get into the habit of taking their folders home at the beginning of each week and returning them with their completed homework on Fridays. These folders should last several months, but you may want to make extras to allow for the inevitable losses.

Suggested Homework Calendar

This homework calendar illustrates how Mind Mover homework assignments can be used to provide a rich and varied homework program for an entire school year. You will, of course, need to adapt these suggestions to your own school schedule and curriculum goals.

Month/Week	Assignment	Material to Be Returned by Students	Optional Homework from Unit 9
SEPTEMBER			
Week 1	Unit 1: Getting Acquainted Letter to Parents All About Me	assignment sheets, story, poem, or picture	
Week 2	This Is My Life	bag of cards	
Week 3	Unit 2: Homework Habits Letter to Parents Homework—When?	assignment sheets, homework schedule	
Week 4	Homework—Where?	assignment sheets, paragraph	
OCTOBER			
Week 1	Unit 3: Spelling Letter to Parents Learning to Learn Spelling Words	assignment sheets	
Week 2	Detecting Spelling Patterns	assignment sheets	
Week 3	Planning a Festival, Celebration, or Fiesta (Halloween)	assignment sheets	Individualized Spelling Sheets with this week's words from your spelling program
Week 4	Halloween Treats	assignment sheets (optional: bag of ten treats)	

Month/Week	Assignment	Material to Be Returned by Students	Optional Homework from Unit 9
NOVEMBER			
Week 1	Unit 4: Time Well Spent Letter to Parents How Long Does It Take? Follow-Up Spelling Test (given in class)	assignment sheets	Spelling Patterns with new rule
Week 2	Television Time	assignment sheets, Blue Ribbon/Turkey List	Making a Presentation (use for book reports)
Week 3	Follow-up sheets for Unit 2: Homework Habits Begin Thanksgiving Turkey Talk	follow-up sheets	
Week 4	Thanksgiving Turkey Talk	assignment sheets, paragraph	
DECEMBER			
Week 1	A Special Gift	assignment sheets, brainstorming record	Individualized Spelling Sheets
Week 2	Planning a Festival, Celebration, or Fiesta (holiday theme)	assignment sheets	Paragraph Planning (holiday theme)
JANUARY			
Week 1	M. L. King Memorial Speech (pp. 218–221)	assignment sheets	Spelling Patterns with new rule
Week 2	M. L. King Memorial Speech (p. 222)	speech notes	
Week 3	Unit 5: Mastering Multiplication Letter to Parents Seeing Double	assignment sheets	
Week 4	The Fives Facts	assignment sheets	Individualized Spelling Sheets
FEBRUARY			
Week 1	Community Valentines	assignment sheets	Individualized Spelling Sheets (used to review fives)
Week 2	Planning a Festival, Celebration, or Fiesta (Valentine's Day or presidents' birthdays)	assignment sheets	Cluster Diagram (the life of Lincoln or Washington)
Week 3	The No-Sweat Nines	assignment sheets	
Week 4	The Perfect Squares	assignment sheets, math games	Individualized Spelling Sheets (used to review nines)

Month/Week	Assignment	Material to Be Returned by Students	Optional Homework from Unit 9
MARCH			
Week 1	The Last Facts	assignment sheets, math games	
Week 2	Arbor Day Tree Study (date varies)	assignment sheets, bag of leaves, tree model	Individualized Spelling Sheets (used to review last facts)
Week 3	Unit 6: Communities Letter to Parents Plant and Animal Communities	assignment sheets	
Week 4	Grandparents' Communities	assignment sheets (optional: letters for you to mail)	Spelling Patterns with new rule
APRIL			
Week 1	Easter Vacation (date varies)		
Week 2	A Parent's Community	assignment sheets, presentation	Individualized Spelling Sheets
Week 3	My Community	community souvenirs	Writing a Letter (reply to grandparents)
Week 4	Bike Town—Planning A Community	community design	
MAY			
Week 1	Unit 7: Business Ventures Letter to Parents Goods and Services	assignment sheets, walking tour record	
Week 2	Testing the Market I	assignment sheets, product or service	Individualized Spelling Sheets
Week 3	Testing the Market II	assignment sheets, product or service	
Week 4	Business Costs Note to Parents	assignment sheets	Spelling Patterns with a new rule
JUNE			
Week 1	Setting a Price	assignment sheets	
Week 2	Open for Business	assignment sheets, sales presentation	
Week 3	My Business Career	assignment sheets, presentation	

GETTING ACQUAINTED

Scope

Two week-long assignments

1. All About Me
2. This Is My Life

Additional Classroom Uses

Math   ■ comparing   ■ graphing   ■ creating and solving story problems

Social Studies   ■ mapping birthplaces   ■ recording oral histories

Oral language   ■ speaking to groups   ■ listening

Written Language   ■ writing short stories and poems   ■ organizing paragraphs   ■ writing and revising rules for a game

Visual Arts   ■ organizing displays of student work

Curriculum Integration

Math   ■ chronological ordering

Social Studies   ■ gaining appreciation of individual differences   ■ informal oral history   ■ making choices   ■ classroom socialization

Oral Language   ■ eliciting feedback   ■ relating personal history   ■ listening

Written Language   ■ gathering and organizing information   ■ writing a poem or paragraph

Fine Arts   ■ illustrating   ■ synthesizing information into a picture

Study Skills   ■ organizing information into clusters   ■ using feedback for revisions   ■ setting patterns for homework

Challenges for GATE Students

■ developing leadership skills   ■ collecting statistics   ■ researching   ■ synthesizing   ■ interviewing   ■ predicting

Unit One

Dear Parent(s):

Your child is about to begin a pair of homework assignments that will help me get to know him or her better. You may be asked to help in different ways, so I thought I would give you a preview of what may be coming up in connection with homework.

In the first assignment, "All about Me," your child will be organizing information using a cluster diagram, a tool that may be unfamiliar to you. A cluster diagram provides a simple yet flexible format for bringing together diffuse information in an easy-to-see manner. Your child will be synthesizing this information by creating a story, poem, or picture about himself or herself.

During this assignment as well as in several future ones, your child may ask you for feedback about his or her work. My experience is that feedback is most useful when it:

- —answers the questions your child asks. It is not so helpful to go beyond what is being asked.
- —is specific or detailed. The statement "You've misspelled several words," is not nearly as helpful as "You need to check the spelling of the words *movies* and *spaghetti*."
- —is nonjudgmental. Information and encouragement produces high-quality work more often than do praise or criticism.

The second assignment, "This Is Your Life," should be fun for both you and your child. Your son or daughter may need help in digging up facts about his or her early years and in arranging those facts in chronological order. Use this moment to look through baby books, photo albums, and other family records to share a bit of family nostalgia with your child. If your son or daughter asks you to play the This Is Your Life Game, you will have a chance to reveal something about your own childhood. Enjoy!

                                    Sincerely,

All About Me

I. Preassessment Considerations

A. Most students will not be familiar with cluster diagrams. It may be helpful to create one as a model in class. See Part II A.

B. Student production of high-quality work will depend largely on how well you communicate your expectations when giving out the assignment. If students know in advance that their work will be displayed, they may take greater pains with their work.

C. The process of getting feedback and using it for revisions in homework may be unfamiliar to students. You may want to discuss revisions in class to ensure that students take these steps seriously.

D. Students will enjoy doing this assignment. The children will find that the most challenging aspects of the assignment are (1) using detail in their work, (2) taking time to produce quality work, and (3) combining the artistic and intellectual aspects of the assignment in a pleasing way.

II. Integration into the Classroom

A. **Enticement Model.** Use yourself as the subject of a cluster diagram on the chalkboard. As you work, talk to students about this format for organizing information. Your class will enjoy learning more about you, including the things that make you happy, your pet peeves, etc.

B. **Displaying Student Work.** Student work can be displayed on walls, organized into a display, or brought together in a class book for browsing. See Part III A for suggestions on using GATE students to help display student work.

C. **Playing Guess Who.** Post students' cluster diagrams with their names covered. Have children try to match each diagram to the student who made it. Ask them how they reached their conclusions.

D. **Writing Assignments.** Have students trade cluster diagrams, and then have each student use his or her partner's diagram to write a paragraph about that student.

E. **Discussion on Feedback.** Discuss with students their experiences in soliciting feedback and using the information they received to revise their work.

III. Extended Activities for GATE Students

A. **Student Displays.** Ask students gifted in visual arts to organize a display of students' stories, poems, and pictures.

B. **Class Profile.** Have a student gifted in math act as class statistician, focusing on just one area of the cluster diagrams such as "foods I love to eat." The statistician should gather information from each student's

Unit One   All About Me

diagram on that topic and make a graph to show the data. You might have several statisticians developing profiles on different topics.

C. **Class Newspaper.** Challenge GATE students to create a class newspaper using students' pictures, poems and stories. They might need help from a parent volunteer to put their paper together.

D. **Biography Reports.** With your GATE students, use the Cluster Diagram in Unit 9 to organize a report on a biographical figure. The students' first step should be to decide what will be the main topics on their cluster diagrams. After collecting information on these topics, students might want to discuss how to use their clusters to help in creating a written or oral report. They should consider ordering their cluster topics and selecting details to include in a report. The final product is not as important as their thinking about the process.

IV. Adapting This Assignment to Your Classroom Program

The cluster diagram used in this assignment is a simple yet powerful tool for helping students to record facts, organize information topically, make connections between ideas, and order their thoughts for writing. Unlike more traditional outlining techniques, clustering does not impose a linear ordering of information and ideas. In addition, a cluster diagram is more flexible than an outline. New topics and information can be added as desired. A cluster is complete on one page, allowing students to look over the whole subject, think about how things relate to each other, and order ideas almost at a glance. Clustering also leads students quite naturally to summarizing ideas and information into key words and phrases, a skill that becomes increasingly important as they move into the upper grades.

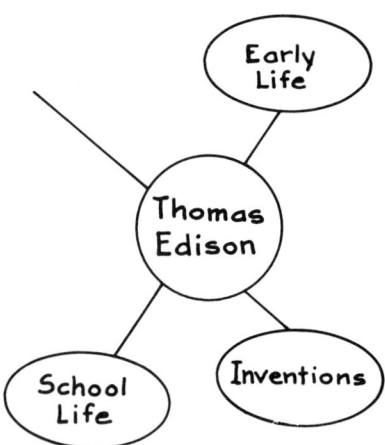

The blank Cluster Diagram in Unit 9 can be used in your classroom in almost any curriculum area. It will particularly be useful in prewriting assignments, in preparing reports, and as a brainstorming tool.*

*For more information on the use of cluster diagrams, see *Writing the Natural Way* by Gabriele Lusser Rico (Los Angeles: J. P. Tarcher, Inc., 1983).

Name

Date Due

All About Me

This week the subject of your homework is you. You will be gathering information about yourself. Then you will choose a way to share some things about yourself with the class.

Skills you will develop
- clustering information
- illustrating
- synthesizing
- getting feedback
- revising your work

What you will need
- pencil
- crayons or marking pens
- paper
- someone to talk with

Before you begin: Read steps 1 through 5, which will help you plan your homework schedule for this week. You will enjoy this assignment most if you do it over several days.

Step 1

Clustering Information about Yourself

This week you will be collecting information about your likes and dislikes, favorite subjects, skills, and other things. One way to keep track of that information is by putting it on a cluster diagram, which is easy to make and easy to read. It allows you to put a lot of information down on paper quickly. You can easily add more information to the diagram whenever you think of something. Here is an example of one boy's cluster diagram about himself.

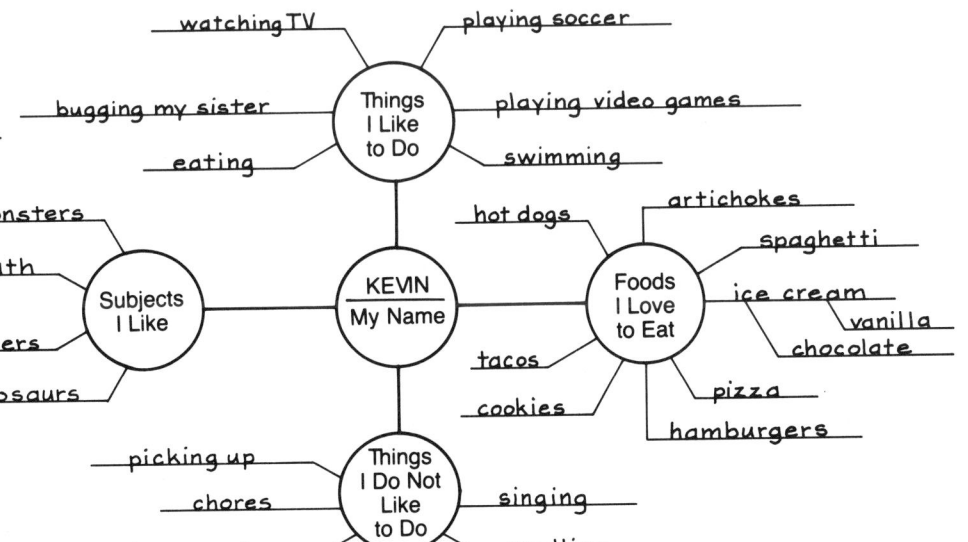

Unit One

Use this cluster diagram to gather information about yourself. Some topic circles are blank. You can fill in your own topics that fit you.

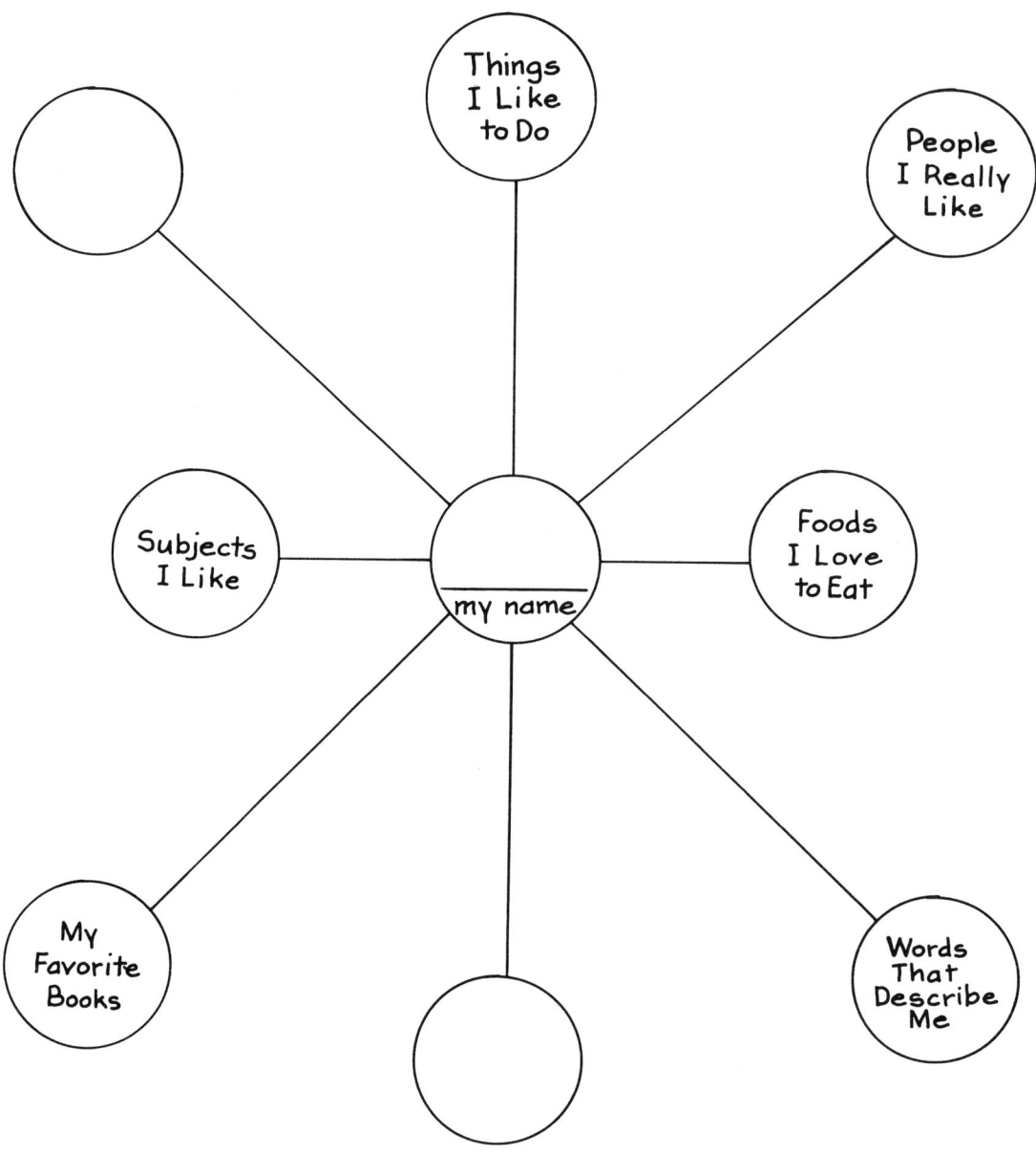

Step 2: Illustrating Your Cluster

Use crayons or marking pens to illustrate your cluster from step 1. The pictures you draw should be simple. You will not have space to illustrate everything on your cluster. Here is how Kevin illustrated his favorite foods.

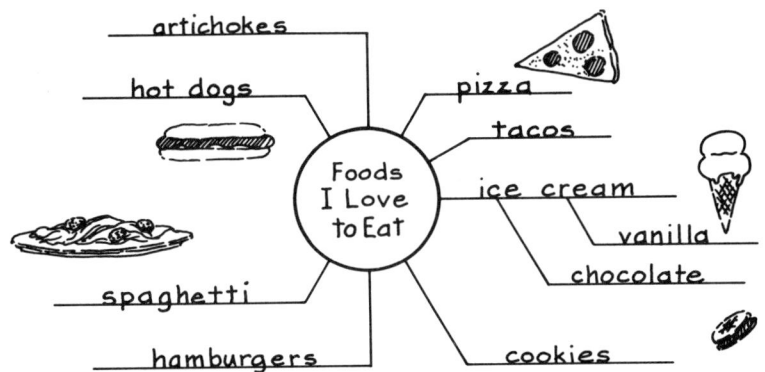

Step 3: Synthesizing Your Information

Now that you have gathered your information, it is time to synthesize it. To synthesize means to put together facts, ideas, or other things to form something new. You will synthesize facts about yourself by creating a poem, story, or picture about yourself. Here are three examples based on Kevin's cluster diagram. Pick the kind of synthesis you like best.

A Story

Sept. 20   Kevin
        My Perfect Day
    On my perfect day I played soccer and went swimming after the game. For lunch I ate pizza. I had hamburgers and a double scoop ice cream cone for dinner. That night I saw a Godzilla movie.

Your story should use information from your cluster diagram. You may want to use the title "My Perfect Day" for your story. Tell what your perfect day would be like.

A Picture

Find a way to bring together many of the illustrations on your cluster to make a picture about yourself.

A Poem

Write a poem about yourself. You can create a cinquain or five-line poem like Kevin's using the following form.

```
        Kevin
     hungry, active
 eating, playing, swimming
   the Godzilla of goalies
       Foodfreak
```

_____
(your name)

_____   _____
(2 words that describe you well)

_____   _____   _____
(3 things you like to do in your free time)

_____   _____   _____   _____
(a new way of seeing yourself using 4 words)

_____
(a good nickname for you)

Step 4 — Getting Feedback

Artists and writers often get feedback from other people about their work. Feedback is simply a response to something they have done. They use the feedback they get to improve their work.

Show your cluster to a parent or other person. Ask the question "Can you think of anything I left out of my cluster?"

Now show your work from step 3 (your story, picture, or poem) to the same person. Tell how you used your cluster to help you with your story, picture, or poem. Explain what part of your work was most difficult for you. Then ask these questions.

- Is there anything in my work you do not understand?
- Have I spelled all my words correctly?
- What do you like best about what I have done in my work?

I talked with _____. (Fill in the name of the person who gave you feedback.)

Step 5: Revising Your Work

The feedback you received may have given you some ideas about how to revise or improve your work. Here are some other suggestions you may not have thought of yet. Put a check in the boxes beside the suggestions that would improve your work. ✓

- ☐ Do my work (story, picture, or poem) over again, using more information from my cluster.
- ☐ Rewrite my story or poem using a typewriter.
- ☐ Revise my work to make it easier to understand.
- ☐ Make my work more attractive by putting it on special paper.
- ☐ Make my work easier to read by correcting misspelled words.
- ☐ Redo my work using marking pens instead of pencil.
- ☐ Make my work easier to read by putting periods at the ends of sentences.
- ☐ Add illustrations, color, or decorations to my poem or story.
- ☐ Make my work neater by copying it on a clean, unwrinkled sheet of paper.
- ☐ Make my picture seem less crowded by redoing it on a larger sheet of paper.
- ☐ Improve my poem or story by using capital leters to begin sentences and proper nouns.
- ☐ Make my work more interesting by including more details.
- ☐ Make my work easier to read by copying it over in my best handwriting.
- ☐ Frame my work by mounting it on a larger sheet of colored paper.

Use your feedback and your checked suggestions to revise your work. Make it your best work. When you have finished, think about how you can carry your work back to school without it getting wrinkled or crumpled.

This Is My Life

I. Preassessment Considerations

A. Children who do not have access to a parent or close family member will find it difficult to collect information on their early years. Encourage such students to use their memories when filling out their cards.

B. This assignment is suitable for all students. The children will find that the most challenging parts of the assignment are (1) ordering cards chronologically, (2) making their cards attractive, and (3) listening carefully to others as they talk about their childhood experiences.

II. Integration into the Classroom

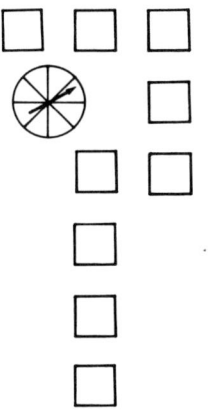

A. **This Is My Life Game.** Group students in pairs to play the game that was part of their homework assignment. They might want to combine their cards for this activity.

B. **Board Game.** Divide the class into groups of from three to five students to play a game. Direct each student to select four or more cards to be arranged with other players' cards in a board game pattern. Be sure the game has a start and a finish. Players might use dice or a spinner to move their markers from card to card. When landing on a new card, a player identifies the card's owner and then makes up a story that fits that person and the subject of the card. Encourage fantasy and fun.

C. **Biography Research Center.** Set up a learning center with biographies of a famous person, a fresh set of This Is My Life cards, and perhaps new cards you have created for this purpose dealing with other aspects of that person's life. Challenge your students to find the information they need to fill out a card about the famous person. When enough cards are filled out, you can use this information to create a class biography of that person by working as a group to order topics and write a few short paragraphs.

D. **Writing Projects.** Have students keep their bags of cards for writing projects throughout the year. The following are two suggestions.

1. Paragraphs: Ask students to select a card from their bags and then cluster ideas that come to mind about that topic. Before they begin to write they should order the items on their clusters and think about a topic sentence. You may want to use Paragraph Planning from Unit 9 to help students organize their paragraphs.

2. Short written pieces: From their bags, have students choose three or more cards that are connected in some way. Give them the cluster diagram from Unit 9 to help them organize their ideas on these topics. Before they begin to write, students should think about how they want to order these topics. Each topic will most likely be the focus of a paragraph. You might also want them to think about opening and concluding sentences for their pieces.

E. **Math Activities.** Because the cards are all the same size, they can be used as one unit of a graph. A class graph on the subject of "Ages We Lost Our First Tooth" might look like this.

Ages We Lost Our First Tooth

age 4 ☐ ☐
age 5 ☐ ☐ ☐
age 6 ☐ ☐ ☐ ☐ ☐
age 7 ☐ ☐ ☐ ☐

Ask comparison questions such as "How many more students lost their first tooth at five than at four?" More difficult questions might be:

"How many children lost their first tooth before the age of seven?"

"How many more children lost their first tooth before the age of six than at age six or older?"

Other ideas for graphing are month of birth, length at birth, and favorite baby food.

III. Extended Activities for GATE Students

A. **Student-Created Game.** Challenge your GATE students to create a game using their cards and other available materials. Give them time to play and revise their game. Extend this activity by having them write down the rules and then test their game on another group of students. As problems and confusions arise, they may need to revise their rules.

B. **Oral Interviews.** Ask your GATE students to organize an interview with a principal or other resource person. For this interview they can use the This Is My Life cards along with other cards they create. The students will have to decide on a format for asking their questions and recording answers while interviewing their guest.

C. **Biographical Speculation.** Many biographies will not contain the specific information asked for in several This Is My Life cards. Have your GATE students read a biography about a famous person and then, based on the information they have, speculate about how that person might have filled out the cards. They might do this by playing the This Is My Life game as a group. As each student draws a card out of the bag, he or she tells how that famous person might have answered the question, giving some reasons for his or her speculations.

Name

Date Due

This Is My Life

Do you remember your first day of kindergarten or where you lost your first tooth? This week you will be looking at your life from the time you were born until now.

Skills you will develop

- making choices
- gathering information
- illustrating
- chronological ordering

What you will need

- pencil
- scissors
- crayons or marking pens
- paper bag

Before you begin: Read steps 1 through 5, which will help you schedule your homework over the next few days.

Making Choices

This week you are going to fill out This Is My Life cards with facts about your own life. To get started, look through the cards on the next few pages. Choose at least twelve that you would like to fill out. Cut them out. You may cut more cards to fill out if you wish.

Gathering Information on Your Life

You may be able to fill out most of your cards without help. Some cards may ask for information that you do not know. Here are some suggestions about where you might find the information you need.

- Ask a parent, grandparent, or older brother or sister.
- Look in your baby book if your parents kept one for you.
- Look in family photo albums for pictures of you when you were younger.
- Read your birth certificate if it is at home.

My birth Date: _____ Day of week: _____ Time of day: _____ Place: _____ _____	Birth Statistics My birth weight: _____ Length: _____ Hair color: _____ Eye color: _____	At the Movies The movie I would most like to see again is _____ _____. I first saw it when I was _____ years old.
First Grade The thing that was hardest for me about first grade was _____ _____ _____.	Snip Snip I had my first haircut when I was __ years old. Where? _____ _____	Happy Birthday The best birthday party I ever had was when I was _____ years old. It was special because _____ _____.
My Invisible Friend I used to have an imaginary friend named _____ when I was _____ years old.	Halloween My best Halloween costume was when I dressed up like a _____ _____ when I was _____ years old.	A Special Pet My family got our pet _____ named _____ _____ when I was _____ years old.
Yummers! Some of my favorite baby foods were _____ _____ _____ _____.	Call for the Doctor I was in the hospital when I was _____ years old. What I remember most about being there was _____ _____.	Moving Day My family moved into our present home when I was _____ years old.

Locomotion	Nicknames	First Day of School
I took my first step when I was _____ years old. I was _____. (Tell where you were.)	When I was _____ years old, I was nicknamed _____.	What I remember most about my first day of kindergarten was _____.

OOPS!	Oh-Oh!	Gifts
My most embarrassing moment was _____. When? _____	The worst punishment I ever had was _____. I was _____ years old.	The best present I ever gave was _____. I gave it to _____ when I was _____ years old.

Four Years Old	T.V.	Say Cheese!
I looked like this when I was four. (Illustrate with a drawing or photo.)	My favorite character on Sesame Street when I was two was _____.	I looked like this when I was a baby. (illustrate with a drawing or photo.)

Nursery School	My Strangest Dream	Summertime
My first nursery school was _____. I began when I was _____ years old.	I dreamed that _____ when I was _____ years old.	The best thing I did last summer was _____.

Toys My favorite toy when I was three was _____.	Ouch! The worst injury I ever had was _____. I was _____ years old when it happened.	Presents The best present I ever received was a _____. I was _____ years old.
My Scariest Moment What happened? _____ _____ When did this happen? _____	Kindergarten What I liked doing best in kindergarten was _____ _____ _____.	Sisters My sister _____ was born when I was _____ years old.
Bye Bye! The farthest I ever went away from home was on a trip to _____ _____ when I was _____ years old.	Books The best book I ever read was _____ _____. I first read it when I was _____ years old.	Brothers My brother _____ was born when I was _____ years old.
Talking The first word I said was _____ when I was _____ years old.	Chompers I lost my first tooth when I was _____ years old. I lost it at _____ _____.	Games. My favorite playground game or activity when I was six was _____ _____.

This Is My Life

Step

Illustrating Your Cards

Make your cards more attractive by adding pictures and color to them. Use crayons or marking pens. Make your pictures fit the information on the cards. There may be some cards that you do not wish to illustrate.

Step

Putting Your Cards in Chronological Order

When you have filled out at least twelve cards, lay them out on a desk or table. Put them in chronological order. This means placing them in order of what happened first, what happened next, and so on. Begin with your birth. Work up toward the things that happened most recently. You may want to ask a parent or other grownup to help you do this.

Once you have the cards in order, number them. Take the first or earliest card in your life and put a number 1 in the circle at the bottom. Write a 2 in the next card in chronological order. Continue until all your cards are numbered.

Step

Playing This Is My Life

Find a paper bag and label it in large letters, THIS IS _____'S LIFE. Write your name in the blank. Put your cards in the bag.

Ask a family member or friend to play This Is My Life with you. The first player begins by taking a card out of the bag. Then that player tells all that he or she can remember about that card's subject. The second player does the same with another card from the bag. If a player has trouble with a card, put it back and take another one. The game is over when all the cards have been taken.

HOMEWORK HABITS

Scope

Two week-long assignments

1. Homework—When?
2. Homework—Where?

Additional Classroom Uses

Math ■ adding time   ■ converting minutes to hours
■ comparing time spent by categories   ■ evaluating time use

Social Studies   ■ developing repect for individual differences

Language ■ writing paragraphs   ■ editing   ■ predicting
■ inferring

Fine Arts   ■ synthesizing generalizations into art or writing

Classroom Management   ■ analyzing study areas

Curriculum Integration

Math ■ learning time awareness and management
■ recording activities in chronological order

Social Studies ■ observing daily activities at home   ■ fitting homework into family schedules   ■ making a contract with a parent

Oral Language   ■ eliciting parental feedback and support

Written Language   ■ categorizing activities   ■ writing paragraphs

Fine Arts   ■ synthesizing information into an artistic, spoken, or written form

Study Skills   ■ scheduling homework time
■ analyzing homework places   ■ establishing homework patterns

Challenges for GATE Students

■ collecting data   ■ analyzing   ■ evaluating   ■ predicting
■ inferring   ■ synthesizing

Dear Parent(s):

Today your child is beginning a unit designed to help him or her establish good homework habits. In the first assignment, "Homework—When?," your son or daughter will be keeping a record of his or her activities from the end of school until bedtime. Some children will need help in remembering what they did each day and at what time they did it. Your child will use this information to create a homework schedule.

Toward the end of this assignment, your child may ask you for feedback on his or her activity record. If you have some concerns about how your child uses after-school time, this would be a good chance to discuss those concerns. You will also be asked to look at your child's homework schedule. If you foresee some schedule conflicts, help your child revise his or her homework schedule to fit in with family commitments.

In the second assignment, "Homework—Where?," your child will be making observations in three possible homework places around your home following his or her homework schedule. Not all children, especially at this age, feel comfortable doing homework alone at a desk in their room. Many prefer a less isolated setting. The purpose of this assignment is to have students test three places and then make an informed decision about which place is best. If your child selects a place to test that you feel is inappropriate, please say so and help him or her choose another place. At the end of the assignment your child will analyze the information gathered and write a paragraph justifying his or her choice. The result may surprise you.

These two assignments reflect my view that homework is an important part of the school experience and deserves to be given high priority in planning after-school activities. If homework is efficiently integrated into your child's schedule, the reward will be (1) the establishment of good home study habits, (2) less tension among family members over homework issues, (3) completion of homework on a consistent basis, and (4) more time for other activities.

Sincerely,

Homework—When?

I. Preassessment Considerations

A. Children who spend their afternoons in day-care centers or who have limited parental support may have special problems in (1) recording their activities, (2) scheduling homework, and (3) getting parental agreement to a homework schedule. You may want to set up a special meeting with such students to explore their concerns and look for possible solutions to their problems.

B. Students who can't tell time may find keeping an activity record frustrating unless they have strong support at home. With such students you may want to limit the assignment to steps 4 and 5.

II. Integration into the Classroom

A. **Motivational Activity.** Project on a screen the activity record from the homework assignment. Fill in one day's activities using your own schedule. Your students may be amazed to find out what you do for them after they go home. Or use the schedule of a favorite fictional character, such as Fern in *Charlotte's Web*. As you work, talk about how students can keep track of their own time.

B. **Discussion.** When students have completed the assignment, ask them if they were surprised by anything in their activity records. You might also want to ask what students found to be the most difficult part of the assignment and whether it was difficult to settle on a schedule both they and their parents could live with.

C. **Show and Tell.** Give your students time to share with their classmates the final synthesis of their homework schedules. You might have one student tally the times chosen for Monday through Thursday on a chalkboard as students reveal their schedules.

III. Extended Activities for GATE Students

A. **Analyzing Activity Records.** Students talented in math might calculate in minutes the time they spent doing activities in each of the categories over the four days covered by their records. Calculators will make this task easier. In many cases students will have to estimate the exact time spent doing a specific chore, eating a snack, etc.

B. **Converting and Comparing Time.** Ask students to convert their total minutes in activity A to hours and minutes. Then have them compare their totals with other students' results. They may be surprised at the variations.

C. **Evaluating Time Use.** Discuss with students what kinds of activities they would like to spend more time doing. What activities would they be willing to cut back on to make this possible? Would their families support them in making such a change?

D. **Making Projections.** Using their activity records as a guide, students can project their total television watching time over a full week, month, and year. A calculator will help in making these calculations.

E. **Writing a Paragraph.** Based on their projections in activity D, each student can write a paragraph that begins as follows:

> If I stopped watching television for a _____
>
> (week, month, or year), I could _____.

Encourage your GATE students to think of fun and fanciful ways to use their newly discovered time.

IV. Adapting This Assignment to Your Classroom Program

A Homework Schedule has been included in Unit 9 to be sent home with students at the beginning of each week. This schedule will help all your students get into the habit of scheduling their homework efficiently. It will prove especially useful to children who have difficulty in dividing their work over several days. There is space on the schedule for students to fill in other homework assignments as well as their Mind Movers assignments.

Name

Date Due

Homework—When?

When is the best time for you to do your homework each day? By the time you finish this assignment you will have a weekly homework schedule.

Skills you will develop
- telling time
- collecting information
- categorizing
- scheduling
- getting feedback
- synthesizing

What you will need
- clock or watch
- pencil
- paper
- marking pens or crayons

Before you begin: Read steps 1 through 6. Go on to steps 2 and 3 before you finish your activity record in step 1.

Step 1

Collecting Information on Your Daily Activities

This week you will be keeping track of what you do after school. This information will help you make a homework schedule.

Use the activity record sheet on page 28 to list the things you do between the end of school and bedtime. Here is one girl's record for Monday.

Monday	
3:00	day care - snack
3:30	day care - games
4:00	soccer practice
4:30	soccer practice
5:00	play with my hamster, clean cage
5:30	set table, watch TV
6:00	eat dinner, help clear table
6:30	play cards with Jeff
7:00	homework
7:30	watch TV
8:00	read

Helpful hints:

- Wear a watch or look at a clock whenever you can to see what you are doing at what time.
- If you can't remember what you did when, ask a parent, brother, or sister for help.
- Fill out your record near the end of Monday, Tuesday, and Wednesday. Don't wait until late Thursday to finish this assignment.

Activity Record Sheet

Monday	Tuesday	Wednesday	Thursday
2:00			2:00
2:30			2:30
3:00			3:00
3:30			3:30
4:00			4:00
4:30			4:30
5:00			5:00
5:30			5:30
6:00			6:00
6:30			6:30
7:00			7:00
7:30			7:30
8:00			8:00
8:30			8:30
9:00			9:00
9:30			9:30

Activity Record Sheet

Step 2

Making a Color Key for Your Record

In the next step you will be categorizing your activities. To do this you need a color key. The key below lists categories of activities. Each category groups together activities that are alike in some way.

With your crayons or marking pens, color in the circle beside each category. Use a different color for each circle.

- ○ *Eating time*
- ○ *Homework time*
- ○ *Television-watching time*
- ○ *Sports time* (time spent practicing and playing sports)
- ○ *Family time* (time spent playing or talking with family members)
- ○ *Personal care time* (time spent bathing, washing hair, etc.)
- ○ *Chore time*
- ○ *Lessons and practice time* (time spent in after-school classes and in practicing for those classes)
- ○ *Free time* (time spent doing anything you want such as reading, playing with friends, listening to records, etc.)
- ○ *Other time* (describe here)_____

Step 3

Categorizing Your Activities

When you finish listing your activities each day, go back over your record once more. For each item on your record, decide which category in your key fits that activity best. Then underline that activity using the color beside that category on your key.

Example: Katie chose to use green on her key for eating time. On her record she underlined after-school snacks and dinner in green. Because she chose yellow for sports time, she underlined her soccer practices in yellow. Katie found that her Girl Scout meeting didn't fit any category. So she wrote *Girl Scouts* beside "other time" on her key. She colored that circle purple and underlined her Girl Scout meeting time with that color.

Step 4 — Making a Homework Schedule

By Thursday you should be ready to make a homework schedule. Look at each day and pick out what you think the best time for homework is that day. You may want to choose a different time for each day. Set aside an hour for homework, even though you will not need that long most days. You may need a full hour now and then. Write the times you chose here.

Monday_____   Tuesday_____

Wednesday_____   Thursday_____

Step 5 — Getting Feedback

Show your activity record and schedule in step 4 to a parent or other grownup. Then ask these questions.

- Is there anything about my activity record that surprises you?
- Do the times I have chosen for my homework fit our family schedule?
- Do you think I should make any changes in my homework schedule?

Use the feedback you get to write a final homework schedule in this box. Then both you and your parent should sign this homework agreement.

Final Homework Schedule Agreement

Monday _____ Tuesday _____ Wednesday _____ Thursday _____

I will try to plan my activities so that these times are set aside for doing my homework.

_____
(Sign your name here.)

I will do my best to see that these times are kept free for my child's homework.

_____
(Ask your parent or other adult to sign here.)

Step 6: Synthesizing a Final Homework Schedule

Think of some new, imaginative way to present your final schedule. It could be a poem, picture, chant, poster, clock, puzzle, or something else you create. Here are two ideas to get you started.

> A Homework Cheer
>
> Monday night from 7:00 to 8:00,
>   Doing homework that's first rate.
> Tuesday night from 8:00 to 9:00,
>   Solving problems with my mind.
> Wednesday afternoon at 4:00,
>   I'm ready for my homework chore.
> Thursday night from 6:00 to 7:00,
>   Homework's done. It feels like heaven.

Homework—Where?

I. Preassessment Considerations

A. Some children may not have a reasonable place for doing homework at home. With such students you might want to suggest other places for doing homework. Suggestions might include school, a public library, a community center, a friend or neighbor's house, a relative's house, or a nearby park or backyard in good weather.

B. If your students have completed "Homework—When?," encourage them to do this week's assignment during their scheduled homework time.

II. Integration into the Classroom

A. **Survey of Homework Places.** After the assignment is completed, divide your class into two groups along one or all of these dimensions.

Those who prefer working alone	vs.	those who like people nearby.
Those who like noise around	vs.	those who like a quiet place.
Those who like to work on a table or desk	vs.	those who like to work on the floor.
Those who like to work in their own room	vs.	those who like to work somewhere other than their own room.

As children shuttle from group to group, discuss the variations in how people like to work, and encourage respect for individual differences.

B. **Sharing Paragraphs.** Divide students into pairs to trade paragraphs. Ask each student to look for a topic sentence, three supporting sentences, and a concluding sentence. If some part of a paragraph is unclear, have partners work together to improve it.

C. **Analyzing and Synthesizing Observations.** Have students look at all the items they marked with blue on their three observation charts. Have each student bring this information together to create a picture or written description of "My Perfect Homework Place." This should not be a particular choice but rather a composite of the best elements of all three places the student observed.

III. Extended Activities for GATE Students

A. **Book of Predictions.** Have GATE students combine your class's homework paragraphs into a book. Following each student's paragraphs, ask the GATE students to add their predictions about where each person might enjoy working in 20 years. Encourage them to make inferences based on present preferences. Examples:

"In 20 years Joshua will be working at his kitchen table with his home computer and cookie jar."

"We predict that Rachel will have a job knitting ski caps while listening to rock music in a big factory."

"In 20 years Juanita will be working in an office by herself writing children's stories."

B. Clue Cards. Ask your GATE students to create a set of clue cards to go with the class's paragraphs about homework places. A card might read as follows.

"This person does homework in a noisy and good-smelling place."

Let other students try to match clue cards with the appropriate paragraphs.

C. Analyzing Classroom Study Places. Give students fresh observation charts to use in your classroom. Have them observe several possible study places and choose the best place to work in the classroom following the same procedure they used at home. Their opinions about where to work may differ from your own in interesting ways.

IV. Adapting This Assignment to Your Classroom Program

Throughout the year you may want to use the Paragraph Planning sheet in Unit 9 to give your students a consistent pattern for organizing paragraphs for writing assignments. This tool becomes more valuable the more it is used.

Name _____

Date Due
Page 1 of 4

Homework—Where?

Where is the best place in your home for you to do homework? You will have a chance to find out in this assignment.

Skills you will develop	**What you will need**
• observing	• pencil
• describing	• paper
• classifying	• crayons or marking pens
• analyzing	• timer or watch
• planning a paragraph	
• synthesizing	
• evaluating	

Before you begin: Read steps 1 through 7. Plan to do the first two steps today.

Finding Homework Places

Walk through your home and find three places where you could do your homework. Each place should have a work space where you can spread out your homework papers and a good light. List the three places here. Examples: Kitchen table, desk in my room, family-room floor.

Place 1: _____   Place 2: _____   Place 3: _____

Observing Place 1

Sit down in place 1 with a watch or timer and a pencil. You will spend the next five minutes making observations about this place. Observations are thoughts about what you see, hear, or feel. Use the chart on page 36 to record your observations.

Now check your watch or set your timer for five mintues and get to work. Try to fill in every box.

Tomorrow you should plan to make observations for place 2 in the same way. The day after tomorrow sit down in place 3 and fill in the third observation chart.

Observation Chart for Place 1

List things you see.	List things you hear.	Tell what people nearby are doing.
List things that take your mind off your work.	Describe your work space.	List your feelings about this place.

Step  **Observing Place 2**

Observation Chart for Place 2

List things you see.	List things you hear.	Tell what people nearby are doing.
List things that take your mind off your work.	Describe your work space.	List your feelings about this place.

Step 4: Observing Place 3

Observation Chart for Place 3

List things you see.	List things you hear.	Tell what people nearby are doing.
List things that take your mind off your work.	Describe your work space.	List your feelings about this place.

Step 5: Analyzing Your Observation Charts

You have collected a lot of information on your observation charts. Now it is time to analyze that information. To analyze something means to study it carefully, to look at all its parts to understand it better. By the time you finish your analysis you should be able to decide which is the best place for doing homework in your home.

Here is one way to do your analyzing. Set all three observation charts in front of you. With a red marking pen or crayon, circle any item on your charts that makes doing homework difficult. You might circle things like radio noise, brothers fighting, a tiny work space, food smells, the TV on, or a cold draft from a window.

With a blue pen or crayon, circle any item that makes doing homework pleasant. Such things might include a comfortable chair, a nearby parent, no noise, lots of noise, or a good feeling about a place.

Step 6: Planning a Paragraph

From your analysis in step 5, decide which place you like best for doing homework. Then, using this chart, plan a paragraph about that place.

Paragraph Planning Chart

1. Write a topic sentence telling where you most like doing your homework.	2. List three reasons for choosing this place.	3. Write a concluding or ending sentence telling how your feel about this homework place.
	a.	
	b.	
	c.	

Step 7: Synthesizing by Writing a Paragraph

Synthesizing means bringing ideas or facts together in a new way. You will do this now by writing a paragraph about your favorite homework place. Use a clean sheet of lined paper for your paragraph. The ideas on your planning chart in step 6 will help you. Here is an example.

Begin with a title.
Skip the line after your title.
Indent the first line of your paragraph.

Can you figure out what to put in your backpack this time?

>   My Homework Place
>
>   I like to do homework on the
> kitchen table best. There is plenty
> of room for my papers. My mom is
> there so I can ask her questions.
> It is not noisy and not too quiet.
> When I work in the kitchen I feel
> warm and happy.

Name

Date Due

Student Homework Follow-up Sheet

A few weeks ago you made up a homework schedule and chose a place to do your homework. The purpose of this follow-up sheet is to help you look at the choices you made then. Give the other follow-up sheet to a parent or adult you live with. When you both have finished answering the questions, compare your answers. If there are problems with your homework place and schedule, work together to solve them.

Evaluating Your Homework Schedule and Place

1. Has the schedule you made up in "Homework—When?" worked well for you most of the time? Check *yes* or *no*, and then answer the questions below your check.

   ☐ Yes   ☐ No

2. Has someone at home helped you follow your schedule?

2. Why is it hard for you to follow your schedule?

3. How could you improve your schedule?

3. How could you make it easier to follow your schedule?

4. Have you been doing your homework in the place you chose in "Homework—Where?" Check *yes* or *no*, and then answer the questions below your check.

   ☐ Yes   ☐ No

5. What do you like about this place?

5. Why haven't you been using that place?

6. Can you think of a better place now for doing homework?

6. Where would you like to do your homework from now on?

Unit Two — Student Homework Follow-up Sheet

Name _____

Date Due _____

Parent Homework Follow-up Sheet

A few weeks ago your child made up a homework schedule and chose a place at home for doing homework. Now is the time for both of you to take a second look at those choices and revise them if necessary. Your child will be answering a similar set of questions. When you both have finished, get together to compare your answers and work out any problems. With practice, your child will become more and more creative at solving problems.

Evaluating Your Child's Homework Schedule and Place

1. Has the schedule your child made up in "Homework—When?" worked well most of the time? Check *yes* or *no*, and then answer the questions below your check.

   ☐ **Yes**   ☐ **No**

2. Have you helped your child follow his or her schedule?

2. Why is it hard for your child to follow his or her schedule?

_____

3. How could the schedule be improved?

3. How could you make it easier for your child to follow the schedule?

_____

4. Has your child been doing homework in the place chosen in "Homework—Where?" Check *yes* or *no*, and then answer the questions below your check.

   ☐ **Yes**   ☐ **No**

5. Are you satisfied with this place?

5. What problems have you found with the place he or she chose?

_____

6. Can you think of a better place for your child to do homework?

6. Can you think of a better place for your child to do homework?

_____

SPELLING

Scope

Two week-long assignments

1. Learning to Learn Spelling Words
2. Detecting Spelling Patterns

Additional Classroom Uses

Study Skills ■ using different learning modalities for memorization
■ comparing short- and long-term memory
■ creating hypotheses

Curriculum Integration

Language ■ using a dictionary to spell   ■ analyzing spelling patterns

Science ■ using the scientific method to create and test hypotheses

Study Skills ■ testing and analyzing learning modalities
■ identifying patterns   ■ using a dictionary
■ developing personalized spelling study plans

Challenges for GATE Students

■ analyzing   ■ applying   ■ hypothesizing   ■ evaluating

Dear Parent(s):

Throughout the year your child will be bringing home assignments that look at spelling in various ways. The assignment "Learning to Learn Spelling Words" introduces children to three modes of learning that exploit auditory memory, kinesthetic (body movement) memory, and visual memory. Most of us learn using all of our senses. Often, however, one of these modes of learning works better than another. At the end of this assignment your child may find that he or she is primarily a visual learner or an auditory learner. If so, you can both use this information to study not just spelling but other things as well more effectively. I encourage you to read your child's assignment for insights into how you learn most efficiently.

The assignment "Detecting Spelling Patterns" looks at spelling from another point of view. We all know that English seems hopelessly irregular when it comes to spelling, but there are patterns of spelling that can be used to improve spelling performance. In this assignment your child will gather words that have specified characteristics and will discover the spelling pattern they follow. I may repeat this assignment several times during the year for different patterns.

Learning to spell is an important communication skill that deserves high priority both at home and in class. In many of the homework assignments I send home, your child will be directed to ask a grownup to check written work for spelling errors. If you spot mistakes, help your child to correct them. When you have doubts about a word you can set a good example for your child by looking it up yourself in a dictionary. By taking time to check words yourself rather than telling your child to do it, you will demonstrate the value you put on correct spelling.

Sincerely,

Learning to Learn Spelling Words

I. Preassessment Considerations

A. The 18 spelling words in this assignment were selected for both their difficulty and their suitability to the three different modes of learning. You may want to substitute harder or easier words for some of your students.

B. This assignment will be helpful for all students. The children will find that following the suggested schedule is the most challenging part of the assignment. You may want to emphasize to students the importance of studying just a few words each night and then testing themselves on the last night of the assignment.

II. Integration into the Classroom

A. **In-class Motivation.** Have students try the following three methods in class to learn three phone numbers or nonsense words.

1. Auditory: Say the numbers or words out loud several times.
2. Kinesthetic: Write the numbers or words in the air several times, using large arm movements.
3. Visual: Write the number or word on a sheet of paper and then look at it for 10 to 15 seconds.

Take time to talk about the terms *auditory, kinesthetic,* and *visual,* explaining how each sense seems to store information in different parts of our brains. You may also want to emphasize that although we all learn things using our auditory, kinesthetic, and visual memories, some of us learn better using one sense rather than another. Finally, test students on the three phone numbers or words. Which learning mode seemed to work best for most of your students?

Note: Some students will be tempted to study the words in this assignment the same way they have always learned spelling words. You may need to encourage them to try these different methods by emphasizing that the main purpose of this assignment is not to memorize 18 new spelling words but to explore how we learn. The knowledge students may gain about how their own minds work has much broader potential application than spelling memorization.

B. **Show and Tell.** When the assignment is completed, ask each child to share a chant, song, picture, typed word list, or other artifact of his or her spelling assignment.

C. **Immediate Follow-up Test.** On the day the assignment comes back, give a brief test using the words students learned. Save this test to compare with a second test to be given in one month.

D. **Delayed Follow-up Test.** Use the follow-up test in class. It is included in this assignment to retest students on their spelling words one month after the assignment. As you compare results with their earlier tests, discuss the difference between long- and short-term memory.

III. Extended Activities for GATE Students

A. Analyzing Learning Modalities. Because many gifted spellers have excellent visual memories, all the study methods in this assignment will have worked well for them. Challenge these students to analyze their strengths and weaknesses further by having them try to learn harder words or strings of numbers.

B. Applying Learning Modalities. Ask your GATE students to use their strongest modality to memorize something. For long or complicated memory tasks students may want to incorporate their second-strongest learning mode. Here are some ideas.

- scout pledge
- poem
- shopping list
- musical piece
- states and capitals
- bones of the body
- counting in another language
- birthdays of family members

IV. Adapting This Assignment to Your Classroom Program

The three "Individualized Spelling Sheets" in Unit 9 can be used regularly to help students study their spelling words at home. Although you will want to have students develop their strongest learning modality, you may also want to vary the activities by occasionally sending home sheets that use other strategies.

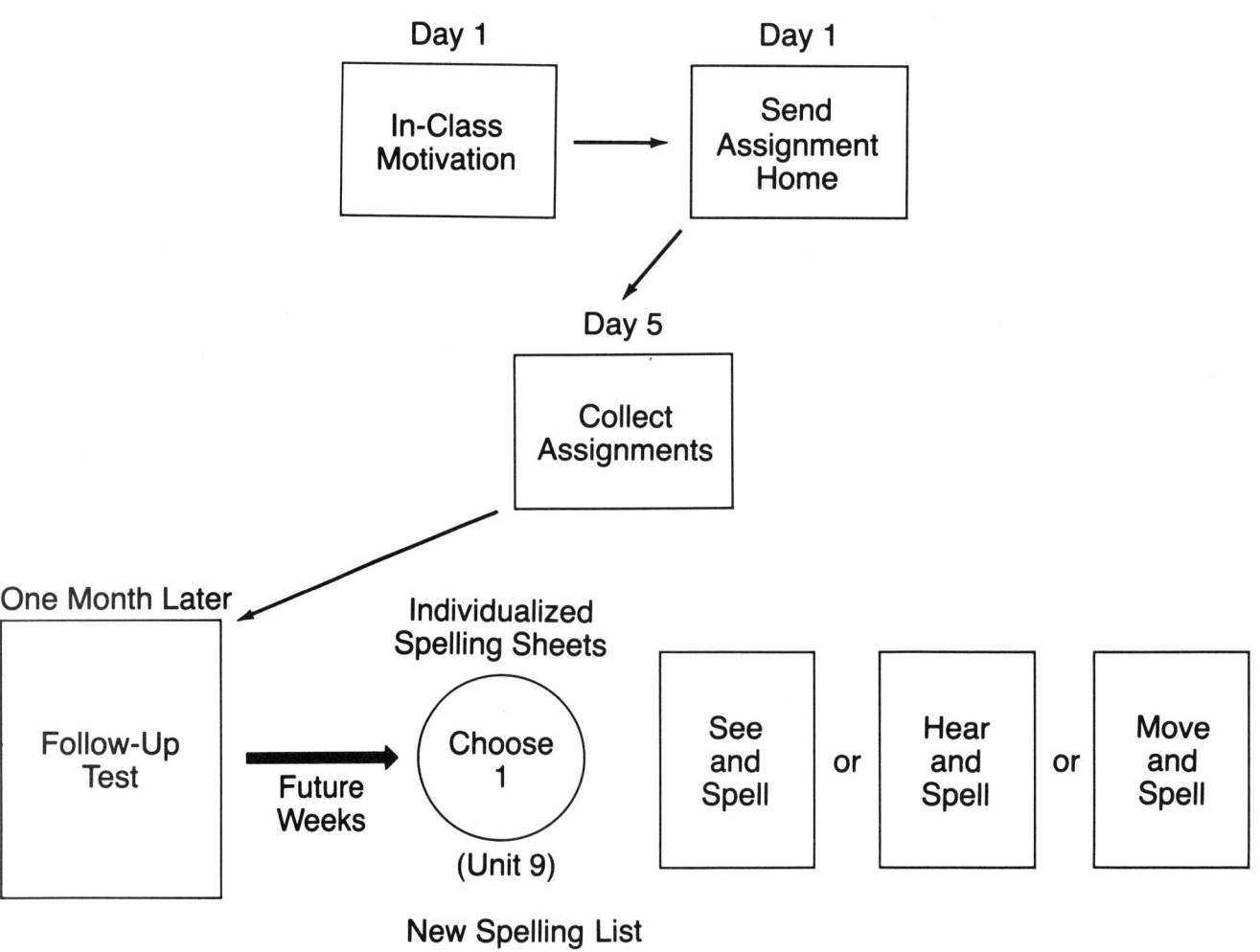

Name

Date Due

Page 1 of 5

Learning to Learn Spelling Words

How do you learn spelling words? Are there other ways that might work better for you? In this assignment you will learn about how you learn.

Skills you will develop

- learning with auditory memory
- learning with kinesthetic memory
- learning with visual memory
- evaluation

What you will need

- pencil
- paper
- (some of the following items) flashlight, typewriter, crayons or marking pens, tape recorder, sugar, shoebox lid, paintbrush, sandpaper

Before you begin: Read steps 1 through 5. Plan to follow this schedule.

Monday: Steps 1 & 2   Wednesday: Step 4
Tuesday: Step 3   Thursday: Step 5

Learning about Learning

Imagine that the telephone company has decided to give your family a new phone number. What would be the best way for you to learn this new number? Check one. ✓

☐ a. Say the number out loud over and over until you remember it.

☐ b. Dial the new number several times until your finger seems to remember it.

☐ c. Look at the number again and again until you remember it.

If you checked *a,* you would have used your auditory memory to learn the new number. Your auditory memory remembers the things you hear.

If you checked *b,* you would have used your kinesthetic memory. Your kinesthetic memory remembers a pattern of body movement.

If you checked *c,* you would have used your visual memory. Your visual memory remembers what you see.

This week you will try all three ways of learning to study spelling words.

Unit Three

Step

Learning Words Using Auditory Memory

Here are five ways to use your ears and your auditory memory to learn spelling words. Choose at least two of them to study the spelling words below.

Spelling Words

ambulance	February	banana
family	sandwich	bicycle

Drum It In

Use your hands or a pencil to create a new rhythm pattern for each word. Example:

r-H-y-t-H-m

Repeat each pattern several times.

Sleep On It

Use a tape recorder to tape yourself spelling each word correctly. Then listen to your tape a few times just before you fall asleep.

Cheer Up

Make up a cheer using each spelling word. Example:

"Poultry, poultry,
that's our cry.
P—O—U—L—T—R—Y."

Yell each cheer several times.

Sing It Out

Use a tune you know or make one up to sing as you spell out each. Example:

Try singing G-R-O-C-E-R-Y to the tune of "Mary Had A Little Lamb."

Sing each word several times while you take a bath or a shower.

Say It Like It Sounds

Say each spelling word aloud as if it were pronounced exactly as it is spelled. Example:

vegetable—Say it like "vegee-table" to remember that second e.

favorite—Say it like "favor-right" to remember the o.

After you say a word as it sounds, spell it correctly. Do this several times for each word.

Which two ideas for studying spelling did you use? _____

Step 3: Learning Words Using Kinesthetic Memory

Here are five suggestions for using your body and kinesthetic memory to learn spelling words. Use at least two to learn the spelling words below.

Spelling Words

friend	children	people
stomach	elevator	except

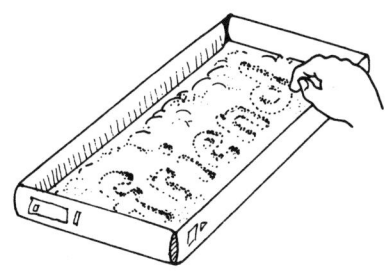

Sweet Talk

Pour one cup of sugar (or salt) into a shoebox lid or shallow pan. Spread the sugar out evenly. With your finger in the sugar, carefully spell out each word.

Water Work

Take a clean paintbrush, a bucket of water, and your spelling words outside. Paint each word in water on the sidewalk, a garage door, or a fence. Make the letters big, and be sure to put them in the correct order.

Back Words

Ask a friend or family member to trace each word on your back with a finger. Guess which word it is. Then spell it back to your friend. Do this until you get all the words right.

Nitty Gritty

Trace each word with your finger on the gritty side of a large sheet of sandpaper. Do this several times for each word.

Leave Your Mark

Find a smooth patch of sand, snow, or dirt. Write out each word in that patch using your hand or a stick. Use your list to spell each word correctly.

Which two ideas for studying spelling did you use? _____

Step 4

Learning Words Using Visual Memory

Here are five ways for using your eyes and your visual memory to learn spelling words. Try using two of them to learn the spelling words below.

Spelling Words

| listen | animal | awful |
| science | important | daughter |

Flashing Lights

Using large letters, write your words on a grocery bag. Take your bag and a flashlight to bed with you. Turn out all the lights. Use your flashlight to light up each word, one letter at a time. Then write each word in light on the ceiling.

Seeing Red

Underline the difficult part of each word on your list. Then write each word in pencil on a piece of paper. Go over the difficult letters in red marking pen or crayon. Example:

S u r p r i s e

Just Your Type

Type out each word on a typewriter, making sure to spell each one correctly. Now type your list a few more times.

Deco-Write

Write out each word using fancy letters. Try several styles of letters for each word.

history

Art Words

Make a picture that uses each word in an interesting way. Be sure you spell the word correctly.

Shoes

Which two ideas for studying spelling did you use? _____

Step 5: Testing Yourself

Ask a friend or family member to give you a spelling test for the words in all three categories.

Auditory Words (step 2)	Kinesthetic Words (step 3)	Visual Words (step 4)
1. _____	1. _____	1. _____
2. _____	2. _____	2. _____
3. _____	3. _____	3. _____
4. _____	4. _____	4. _____
5. _____	5. _____	5. _____
6. _____	6. _____	6. _____

Correct each test carefully.

Which group of words gave you the most trouble on your test? Check one box.

☐ a. Auditory words
☐ b. Kinesthetic words
☐ c. Visual words
☐ d. None of them
☐ e. All of them

Learning to Learn Spelling Words

Name _____

Learning to Learn Spelling Follow-Up Test

About a month ago, you tried three different approaches to learning spelling words. You tested yourself to find out which method worked best for you. At that time you were testing your short-term memory, which is the part of your memory that holds information you have learned recently.

Some of the information in our short-term memories is forgotten soon after we learn it. Other information is moved to our long-term memories, where we will be able to remember it for a long time. Today you will be able to test yourself again on the words you learned last month. This may help you find out which way of learning helps you put spelling words into your long-term memory. Your teacher will give you your spelling words.

Auditory Words	Kinesthetic Words	Visual Words
1. _____	1. _____	1. _____
2. _____	2. _____	2. _____
3. _____	3. _____	3. _____
4. _____	4. _____	4. _____
5. _____	5. _____	5. _____
6. _____	6. _____	6. _____

Correct each test carefully.

Which group of words gave you the most trouble on your test? Check one box. ✓

☐ a. Auditory words   ☐ d. None of them
☐ b. Kinesthetic words   ☐ e. All of them
☐ c. Visual words

Of all the ways you studied spelling a month ago, which do you think worked best in getting your words into long-term memory?

_____

Detecting Spelling Patterns

I. Preassessment Considerations

The first three steps in this assignment—collecting words, checking spellings, and analyzing patterns—can be done by all students. The last three steps involve writing, testing, and applying hypotheses and may be difficult for some children. Your alternatives are to send the first three steps home and complete the assignment in class or to pair stronger and weaker students to finish the last steps.

II. Integration into the Classroom

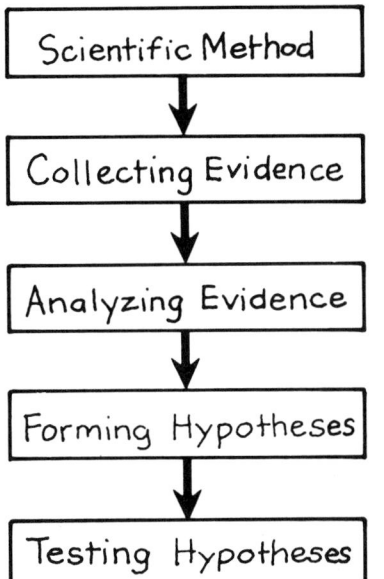

A. **Brainstorming Word Sources.** When giving out this assignment, spend a few moments brainstorming about sources of interesting words. Be sure students understand that they will be looking for /k/ words in which the initial *c* or *k* is followed by a vowel.

B. **Combining Word Lists.** Set up classroom word lists, and have students contribute their most interesting words all week long. You may enjoy talking about the obscure or curious words as they are added to the lists.

C. **Writing a Hypothesis.** If you did not send home steps 4 through 6, use your classroom lists to write a spelling hypothesis in class. Ask students to test this hypothesis with words from their lists.

D. **Applying Spelling Patterns.** Complete step 6 in class if you did not send it home. Words with *a* as the second letter may pose problems for some students. Those included in step 6 follow the common pattern of beginning with *c*. There are a few exceptions to this rule, however, such as *kangaroo* and *kayak*. (See IIIA.)

E. **Spelling Bee with /k/ Words.** Use your students' word lists and words you collect for a spelling bee. Instead of spelling each word, however, students should listen closely and then tell whether the word begins with *c* or *k*. The more unusual the word, the harder this distinction becomes.

III. Extended Activities for GATE Students

A. **Hypothesizing about /ka/ Words.** Have GATE students collect /ka/ words from a classroom dictionary. Then ask them to suggest hypotheses about why these words seem to violate the normal English spelling patterns. Students may need to consult an adult dictionary that includes information on word origins to test their hypotheses.

B. **Keeping a Pattern Journal.** Help your GATE students create their own pattern journals. Each time they discover a pattern in art, language, spelling, math, science, nature, or daily life they should record it in their journals.

IV. Adapting This Assignment to Your Classroom Program

Now that your students have learned to apply the scientific method (collecting and analyzing evidence, creating and testing hypotheses) to spelling patterns, repeat this assignment using Spelling Patterns from Unit 9. The following are some of the patterns you might have your students pursue.

A. Words that begin with a soft *g* followed by a vowel.
Examples: *Germ, giant, gypsy.*
Pattern: A soft *g* can be followed only by the vowels *e, i,* or *y.*

B. Words that begin with a soft *c* followed by a vowel.
Examples: *Cereal, circle, cycle.*
Pattern: A soft *c* can be followed only by the vowels *e, i,* or *y.*

C. Words with the letter combinations *cei* or *cie.*
Examples: *Receive, ancient.*
Pattern: The letter *e* comes before *i* when the *c* sounds like *s.*
The letter *i* comes before *e* when the *c* has the *sh* sound, as in *ancient.*
(There is one exception to the rule: the word *financier.*)

D. Words with the letter combinations *ei* or *ie* where those letters have a long *e* sound.
Examples: *Field, ceiling, niece.*
Pattern: Most of these words are spelled with *ie.* A soft *c* is followed by *ei.*
(There are exceptions, like *seize, either,* and *leisure.*)

E. Words that end with a consonant followed by *y* and their plurals.
Example: *duty* and *duties.*
Pattern: The *y* changes to *i,* and *es* is added to make the plural.

F. Words that end with a vowel followed by *y* and their plurals.
Example: *Boy* and *boys.*
Pattern: The *y* is left alone, and *s* is added to make the plural.

Name

Date Due

Detecting Spelling Patterns

Are you ready to be a spelling detective? Your job is to find spelling patterns that can help you become a better speller.

Skills you will develop

- collecting words
- categorizing
- using a dictionary
- analyzing patterns
- making hypotheses
- testing hypotheses
- applying spelling patterns

What you will need

- pencil
- places to find words
- dictionary

Step 1

Collecting the Evidence

This week's spelling mystery concerns words that start with the /k/ sound. Some of those words start with the letter *c*. Others begin with the letter *k*. Did you know that there is a spelling pattern to many of these words? Once you have discovered that pattern, you can use it to become a better speller.

Like any detective, you must begin by collecting evidence. You will need to collect 30 /k/ sound words. The second letter in each word you collect should be a vowel: *a, e, i, o, u* or *y*. Half of the words should begin with *k*, such as *key* or *kick*. The other 15 should begin with *c*, such as *corn* or *cat*.

You can look for words in lots of places. Listen to people talking for ideas. Look in books, newspapers, and magazines. Check the labels on cans and cereal boxes. List the words you find on the following evidence sheet.

Unit Three

Spelling Detective Evidence Sheet

/k/ sound words that begin with *c* followed by a vowel:

1._____
2._____
3._____
4._____
5._____
6._____
7._____
8._____
9._____
10._____
11._____
12._____
13._____
14._____
15._____

/k/ sound words that begin with *k* followed by a vowel:

1._____
2._____
3._____
4._____
5._____
6._____
7._____
8._____
9._____
10._____
11._____
12._____
13._____
14._____
15._____

Using a Dictionary to Spell Correctly

Your detective work depends on good, solid evidence. Are all the words on your evidence sheet spelled correctly? If you are not sure of some words, look them up in a dictionary at home or at school.

Show your list to a good speller. Ask that person to point out any spelling mistakes. Correct those words before going on.

Step 3

Analyzing Your Evidence

Good detectives do more than gather evidence. They also analyze it, which means studying the evidence to see how it all fits together.

The words on your list are alike in some way. Can you spot the spelling pattern? It may help to say the words aloud and listen to how they sound. You may also want to circle groups of letters that appear in more than one word. Here is an example.

      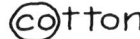

Look at your list of words that begin with *c*. Describe the pattern you see.

_____

_____

Look at your list of words that begin with *k*. Describe the pattern you see.

_____

_____

Step 4

Writing a Spelling Hypothesis

As detectives analyze their evidence they try to think up a theory or hypothesis to explain what they have found. A hypothesis is a good guess about what seems to be true. It is based on the evidence a person has. More evidence may help prove that the hypothesis is true, or new evidence may show that a hypothesis is not correct.

Use your analysis of spelling patterns in step 3 to complete this spelling pattern hypothesis.

Spelling Hypothesis

Most words that begin with the /k/ sound start with the letters *c* or *k*. When the first letter is *c* followed by a vowel, the vowel is probably the letter __ or __. When the first letter is *k* followed by a vowel, the vowel is most likely to be the letter __ or __.

Testing Your Hypothesis

Is your hypothesis true? To test it, gather new evidence. Find 10 more /k/ sound words with a vowel as the second letter. List them here.

1. _____   6. _____

2. _____   7. _____

3. _____   8. _____

4. _____   9. _____

5. _____   10. _____

Do all these words fit your hypothesis? If some do not, you may want to go back to step 4 and change your hypothesis.

Applying Spelling Patterns

Here are several words that begin with the /k/ sound. Use your spelling patterns to supply the correct first letter.

____antaloupe—a kind of melon

____ettledrum—a large drum

____itten—a young cat

____oconut—the large fruit of a palm tree

____illjoy—a gloomy person who makes others feel bad

____ernel—the soft part of corn

____omplexion—the color and look of a person's skin

____aribou—a kind of deer

____ulprit—a person who has done something wrong

____uckoo—a bird with a call that sounds like its name

____etchup—the best thing to put on a hamburger

____atsup—still the best thing to put on a hamburger

____ockatoo—a kind of parrot

____indergarten—your first year in elementary school

____omedian—a person who makes people laugh

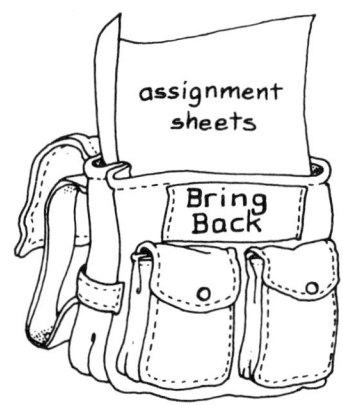

TIME WELL SPENT

Scope

Two week-long assignments.

1. How Long Does It Take?
2. Television Time

Additional Classroom Uses

Math ■ comparing elapsed times

Oral Language ■ discussing speed and quality ■ developing criteria

Written Language ■ writing critiques

Classroom Management ■ applying time measurement skills to classroom activities

Curriculum Integration

Math ■ measuring elapsed time ■ averaging

Social Studies ■ timing family activities ■ evaluating time use

Oral Language ■ interviewing

Written Language ■ identifying and analyzing criteria ■ summarizing ■ creating rating charts

Science ■ experimenting with timed activities

Fine Arts ■ evaluating television programs

Study Skills ■ analyzing time use

Challenges for GATE Students

■ analyzing ■ synthesizing ■ evaluating
■ applying ■ statistical analysis
■ classroom dramatic activities

Unit Four

Dear Parent(s):

Your child is about to begin a pair of homework assignments that look—from very different viewpoints—at how we spend time. In "How Long Does It Take?" your child will learn how to measure elapsed time by timing a variety of everyday activities. Some of the activities, such as shaving in the morning or grocery shopping, may involve you. At the end of the assignment your son or daughter will consider how to speed up an activity and whether doing it faster means doing it better. Quality is not often the result of speed.

The issue of quality is central to the second assignment, called "Television Time." As part of this assignment your child will develop his or her own criteria for judging the quality of television programs. He or she will choose three shows to evaluate—a good show, a poor show, and one never watched before. You will be asked to choose a fourth program for your child to evaluate. This is your chance to extend your son's or daughter's viewing horizons beyond the usual fare, so select carefully.

If the quality of television watched by your family is of concern to you, you might want to extend this assignment beyond this week. Make copies of the rating charts or make up a rating scheme of your own. Ask the entire family to help create viewing criteria and rate shows by these standards. It may take time, but after a while you may all become more discriminating in what you watch.

Sincerely,

How Long Does It Take?

I. Preassessment Considerations

A. All children who can tell time will enjoy this assignment. Students whose parents are largely unavailable may need some suggestions about other adults whose activities they might time. Or you might leave out step 3 of the assignment for these students.

B. You may need to supply a watch or clock for the occasional student who lacks a timepiece at home.

C. The children will find that the most challenging activities in this assignment are analyzing and evaluating whether faster is better.

II. Integration into the Classroom

A. **Measuring Elapsed Time.** Before sending this assignment home, go through step 1 with the whole class. Have children read the same five pages. Then try timing one of the activities in step 4 to spark enthusiasm.

B. **Comparing Times.** When the assignment comes back to class, pair each student with another child who timed at least one of the same activities. Have them compare their times and come up with a list of reasons to explain why times might vary considerably.

Examples: Electric vs. blade razor for shaving.
Microwave vs. conventional oven for cooking.
Time of day when shopping.
Distance from school.
Size of lunch.

C. **Evaluating Times.** Have each pair consider the following questions for the activity they are comparing. Could this activity be done better if more time were taken? How? Would it be better to do this activity in less time? Why or why not?

III. Extensions for GATE Students

A. **Time Equations.** Ask your GATE students to cut out their completed time cards and arrange them in order from the activity taking the least time to that taking the most. Challenge students to arrange selected cards into equations in which both sides add up to an equal amount of time. Then write out the equation as a statement: "I can _____ in the same amount of time it takes to _____."

How long does it take you to get dressed in the morning?	How long does it take you to brush your teeth doing a really good job?	How long does it take to make breakfast or dinner? (Circle one.)
Your estimate ___:09 hr. min.	Your estimate ___:06 hr. min.	Your estimate ___:17 hr. min.
Ending time 7:10	Ending time 7:15	Ending time 7:15
− Starting time 7:00	− Starting time 7:10	− Starting time 7:00
Elapsed time ___:10	Elapsed time ___:05	Elapsed time ___:15

"It takes me as long to brush my teeth and get dressed for school as it takes my mother to fix breakfast."

B. **Time Graphs.** Have a GATE student create a graph showing the distribution of times students recorded in step 1. Additional graphs could be made for other activities timed by several students.

C. **Classroom Timekeeping.** Appoint one student to time certain classroom activities that you would like to see speeded up.

Examples: Quieting down in the morning.
Cleaning up after art.
Getting ready for spelling.

Use the initial times to help your class set achievable goals. Then have your timekeeper time these activities on a regular basis and graph the class's progress.

Name

Date Due
Page 1 of 6

How Long Does It Take?

Do you know how long it takes you to brush your teeth? In this assignment you will find out how long it takes to do many everyday activities.

Skills you will develop

- measuring time
- estimating elapsed time
- analyzing
- evaluating

What you will need

- pencil
- watch, clock, or stopwatch
- cooperative adult

Before you begin: Read steps 1 through 6. Find an adult who will work with you on your homework this week.

Step 1 — Learning to Measure Elapsed Time

This week you will be finding out how long it takes to do ordinary activities. To do this, you need to know how to measure elapsed time. Elapsed time is the time that goes by from the start of something to its finish. The activities are listed in boxes like the one on the next page. As you fill out this card now, you will learn how to measure elapsed time.

Unit Four

1. Begin by reading the question at the top of the card.
2. Next, guess or estimate how long it will take you to do this activity. Write your estimate here.
3. Open your book to the page where you will begin reading. Look at a clock or watch. Write down the exact time you begin reading on the line marked "Starting time." (*Hint:* Write down the hour and minutes. Don't worry about seconds. Round off to the nearest minute.)

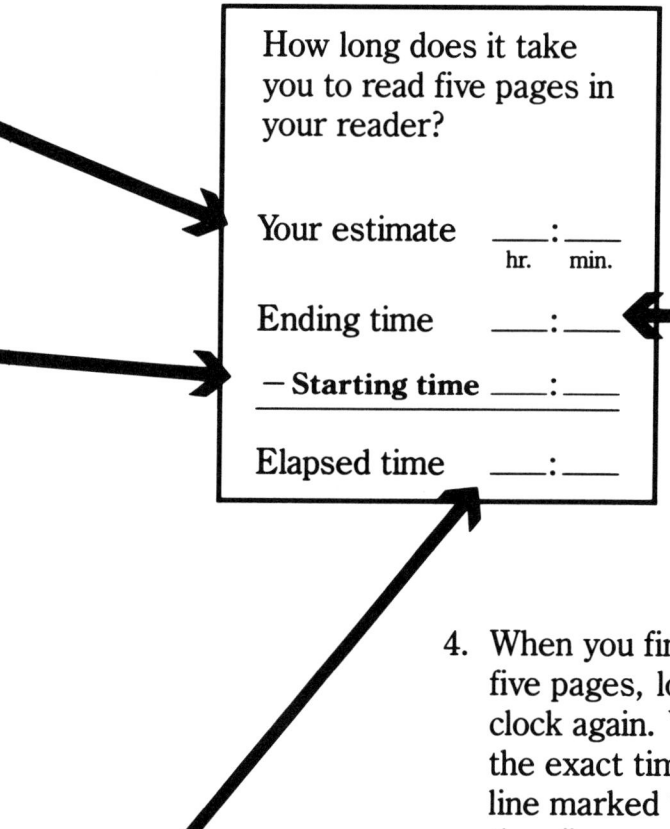

4. When you finish reading five pages, look at the clock again. Write down the exact time on the line marked "Ending time."
5. Subtract your starting time from your ending time. The answer is the amount of time it took you to do this activity. Put it on the "Elapsed time" line.
6. Compare your estimate with the actual time it took you to read five pages. How good a guess did you make?

EXTRA: You can also use a stopwatch or digital watch that works like a stopwatch to time your activities. Start the stopwatch when you begin. Stop it as soon as you finish. The time on the stopwatch is your elapsed time. Round it off to the nearest minute and write it on the "Elapsed time" line. Leave the "Starting time" and "Ending time" lines blank.

Step 3: Timing Everyday Activities

Time yourself doing at least three of the activities in the boxes on this page. You can do more than three if you want to. If you had trouble measuring elapsed time in step 1, ask a friend or grownup to help you.

How long does it take you to get dressed in the morning? Your estimate ___:___ hr. min. Ending time ___:___ − Starting time ___:___ Elapsed time ___:___	How long does it take you to brush your teeth doing a really good job? Your estimate ___:___ hr. min. Ending time ___:___ − Starting time ___:___ Elapsed time ___:___	How long does it take you to make your bed? Your estimate ___:___ hr. min. Ending time ___:___ − Starting time ___:___ Elapsed time ___:___
How long does it take you to get from your home to school by _____? (foot, bike, bus, car) Your estimate ___:___ hr. min. Ending time ___:___ − Starting time ___:___ Elapsed time ___:___	How long does it take you to eat lunch at school? Your estimate ___:___ hr. min. Ending time ___:___ − Starting time ___:___ Elapsed time ___:___	How long does it take you to walk around the block? Your estimate ___:___ hr. min. Ending time ___:___ − Starting time ___:___ Elapsed time ___:___
How long does it take you to set the table or to clear the table? (Circle one.) Your estimate ___:___ hr. min. Ending time ___:___ − Starting time ___:___ Elapsed time ___:___	How long does it take you to peel an orange or an apple or a potato? (Circle one.) Your estimate ___:___ hr. min. Ending time ___:___ − Starting time ___:___ Elapsed time ___:___	_____ _____ (Fill in your own idea.) Your estimate ___:___ hr. min. Ending time ___:___ − Starting time ___:___ Elapsed time ___:___

Step 3: Timing an Adult's Activities

All the activities on this page are things adults do. Sit down with your cooperative adult and pick out three things to time together.

How long does it take to shave in the morning?
 	
Your estimate ___:___
   hr. min.
 	
Ending time ___:___
− Starting time ___:___
 	
Elapsed time ___:___
	How long does it take to iron a shirt or blouse?
	
	Your estimate ___:___
	   hr. min.
	
	Ending time ___:___
	− Starting time ___:___
	
	Elapsed time ___:___
		How long does it take to read the paper?
		
		Your estimate ___:___
		   hr. min.
		
		Ending time ___:___
		− Starting time ___:___
		
		Elapsed time ___:___

How long does it take to mow the lawn?
 	
Your estimate ___:___
   hr. min.
 	
Ending time ___:___
− Starting time ___:___
 	
Elapsed time ___:___
	How long does it take to make breakfast or dinner? (Circle one.)
	
	Your estimate ___:___
	   hr. min.
	
	Ending time ___:___
	− Starting time ___:___
	
	Elapsed time ___:___
		How long does it take to travel to work in the morning?
		
		Your estimate ___:___
		   hr. min.
		
		Ending time ___:___
		− Starting time ___:___
		
		Elapsed time ___:___

How long does it take to shop for groceries from the time you enter the market until you leave it?
 	
Your estimate ___:___
   hr. min.
 	
Ending time ___:___
− Starting time ___:___
 	
Elapsed time ___:___
	How long does it take to fill the car with gas from the time you enter a gas station until you leave it?
	
	Your estimate ___:___
	   hr. min.
	
	Ending time ___:___
	− Starting time ___:___
	
	Elapsed time ___:___
		_____
		_____
		(Fill in your own idea.)
		
		Your estimate ___:___
		   hr. min.
		
		Ending time ___:___
		− Starting time ___:___
		
		Elapsed time ___:___

How Long Does It Take?   Unit Four

Step 4 — How Long Can You Do Things?

The activities on this page are things you can do. But for how long? You'll never know until you time yourself. Pick out at least three activities to try. You may want to do some activities more than once. Report your best time.

How long can you make an ice cream cone last? Your estimate ___:___ 　　　　　　　　hr.　min. Ending time　　___:___ − Starting time ___:___ Elapsed time　　___:___	How long can you hold your breath? Your estimate ___:___ 　　　　　　　　hr.　min. Ending time　　___:___ − Starting time ___:___ Elapsed time　　___:___	How long can you jump rope without missing? Your estimate ___:___ 　　　　　　　　hr.　min. Ending time　　___:___ − Starting time ___:___ Elapsed time　　___:___
How long can you bounce a ball without missing? Your estimate ___:___ 　　　　　　　　hr.　min. Ending time　　___:___ − Starting time ___:___ Elapsed time　　___:___	How long can you stand on your head? Your estimate ___:___ 　　　　　　　　hr.　min. Ending time　　___:___ − Starting time ___:___ Elapsed time　　___:___	How long can you jog without stopping? Your estimate ___:___ 　　　　　　　　hr.　min. Ending time　　___:___ − Starting time ___:___ Elapsed time　　___:___
How long can you stare at someone without blinking? Your estimate ___:___ 　　　　　　　　hr.　min. Ending time　　___:___ − Starting time ___:___ Elapsed time　　___:___	How long can you go without saying _____? (Pick a word that you use a lot or that bothers your parents.) Your estimate ___:___ 　　　　　　　　hr.　min. Ending time　　___:___ − Starting time ___:___ Elapsed time　　___:___	_____ _____ (Fill in your own idea.) Your estimate ___:___ 　　　　　　　　hr.　min. Ending time　　___:___ − Starting time ___:___ Elapsed time　　___:___

Step 5 — Analyzing One Activity

Of all the activities you timed, which one would you like to do faster? _____

_____

Think about all the steps involved in that activity. Then list the things that could save time in doing it. (Examples: Move more quickly; don't waste time fooling around; do the steps in a better order; put the things you need for it away in the proper place so you can find them quickly.)

_____

_____

_____

Step 6 — Evaluating Whether Faster Is Better

What would be the advantages of doing the activity you chose in step 5 faster? What would you gain by doing it in less time? _____

_____

_____

What would be the disadvantages? What might you lose by doing it faster? _____

_____

_____

_____

What could you improve, if anything, by doing this activity more slowly? _____

_____

For the activity you chose, do you think faster is better?____
Why or why not? _____

_____

Television Time

I. Preassessment Considerations

A. To complete this assignment, students must have access to a television set and some family cooperation so that they can watch the programs they have chosen to evaluate.

B. This assignment is suitable for all your students. The children will find that the most challenging parts of the assignment are choosing rating criteria and evaluating programs.

II. Integration into the Classroom

A. **Discussing Criteria.** Before you send this assignment home, have your class discuss and list the characteristics they look for in books they enjoy. Choose four favorites and have students rate a book they have all read on a scale like that used in step 4.

B. **Compiling Ratings.** When students bring their TV ratings back to class, compile a list of blue-ribbon programs and turkeys. Your class will have to decide what rating qualifies a program for either list. Post these lists in the classroom in an interesting way.

To be a turkey a program must
_____
_____
_____
_____

This is our vote for the turkey of the week.
_____

To be a winner a program must
_____
_____
_____
_____

This is our vote for the winner of the week.
_____

C. **Writing Critiques.** Ask students to choose their favorite of the four shows they reviewed for writing a critique. The Paragraph Planning chart in Unit 9 will help students organize their thoughts. Suggest that they begin with a simple topic sentence of the following type.

"I think _____ is a very good television show."

D. **Television Newsletter.** Combine your students' critiques to create a television newsletter featuring your class's favorite shows. Be sure to send copies home for families to enjoy. You may want to follow up with another edition featuring critiques of the worst-rated shows.

E. **Writing Fan Letters.** Students may enjoy sending a letter to the appropriate local television station or network headquarters about their favorite programs. The body of each letter should be the reasons the student likes that show. Students might also want to include any questions they have about the programs. The sections Writing a Letter and Addressing an Envelope in Unit 9 will make this task less formidable.

III. Extensions for GATE Students

A. **Math Activities.** Gifted math students can analyze and compile class ratings in many different ways. Here are a few ideas.

1. List all rated programs in order according to which was rated most often down to those programs rated only once.
2. Find the average rating of each show rated by two or more students.
3. Tally the characteristics used by students in their ratings to find out which criteria were selected most often for evaluating programs.
4. Use a bar graph to show the distribution of ratings (i.e., how many programs were rated 1,2,3,4, and 5).
5. List all the "Parent's Choice" programs and find out how many times each show was chosen and what the average rating of each one was.

B. **Creating a Hit Show.** Challenge creative and performance-oriented students to create a television program their class would like based both on the characteristics students used in their evaluations and which programs were highly rated by many students. Have the students test their show in front of the class.

C. **Turkey Reruns.** Your GATE students with well-developed senses of humor and a flair for the ridiculous will enjoy creating an episode of one of the lowest rated shows to perform in class. They might even want to include some of the world's worst commercials.

Name

Date Due
Page 1 of 4

Television Time

What makes a good television program better than a bad one? You may be able to answer this question as you evaluate several television shows.

Skills you will develop

- interviewing
- collecting information
- analyzing
- evaluating

What you will need

- pencil
- paper
- television schedule for this week
- television set
- cooperative adult

Before you begin: Read steps 1 through 6. Begin steps 1, 2, and 3 as soon as you can.

Step 1

Analyzing Television Programs

Think about the television shows you have watched recently. Which ones were blue-ribbon winners? Which were terrible turkeys? What made the difference?

While you think about this, take a piece of lined paper and fold it in half to form two columns. Draw a prize ribbon at the top of the left column. Draw a turkey at the top of the right column. Under the ribbon list the qualities that you find in good television shows. List the characteristics of poor TV shows under the turkey. Here is an example.

🎀	🦃 Amy
makes me laugh	jokes are stupid
I like the characters	too much singing
I learn things	nothing happens
keeps moving	people act dumb
leaves me feeling happy	same thing every show
takes me new places	people seem phony
surprises me	crummy animation

Unit Four

Step 2 — Interviewing about Television Programs

Talk to at least two people about what they like and do not like in television programs. Add their answers to your own on your ribbon/ turkey list.

Write here the names of the two people you talked with.

1. _____ 2. _____

Step 3 — Selecting Important Qualities

Look through all the good qualities you have listed under your blue-ribbon shows. In your opinion, which ones are most important? Circle the four qualities you look for most in a good program.

Think about how you can summarize each of those four qualities in just one or two words. For example, "I like the characters" can be summarized in the two words "likeable characters."

List your summaries of the four qualities you circled.

1. _____ 3. _____

2. _____ 4. _____

Step 4 — Creating Rating Charts

Write these four qualities on the Good Show Rating Chart. Here is how Amy's chart looked.

Good Show Rating Chart

Program_____

Qualities	Ratings
funny	1 2 3 4 5
likeable characters	1 2 3 4 5
surprising	1 2 3 4 5
leaves me happy	1 2 3 4 5
Overall rating	◯ ÷ 4 = ☐

Next, write the same qualities on the other three charts.

Good Show Rating Chart

Program _____

Qualities	Ratings
	1 2 3 4 5
	1 2 3 4 5
	1 2 3 4 5
	1 2 3 4 5
Overall rating	◯ ÷ 4 = ☐

Poor Show Rating Chart

Program _____

Qualities	Ratings
	1 2 3 4 5
	1 2 3 4 5
	1 2 3 4 5
	1 2 3 4 5
Overall rating	◯ ÷ 4 = ☐

New Show Rating Chart

Program _____

Qualities	Ratings
	1 2 3 4 5
	1 2 3 4 5
	1 2 3 4 5
	1 2 3 4 5
Overall rating	◯ ÷ 4 = ☐

Parent's Choice Rating Chart

Program _____

Qualities	Ratings
	1 2 3 4 5
	1 2 3 4 5
	1 2 3 4 5
	1 2 3 4 5
Overall rating	◯ ÷ 4 = ☐

Rating Chart Key

1. About the worst I've ever seen.
2. A little worse than most shows.
3. About the same as most shows I watch.
4. Better than most shows.
5. About the best I've ever seen.

Step 5

Choosing Programs to Evaluate

Sit down with a television schedule for this week. From all the programs you are allowed to watch, pick out one you think is the best. Write the name of that show at the top of the Good Show Rating Chart. Choose a poor show to watch and write its name on the Poor Show Rating Chart. Finally, pick out a show you have never watched before. Write its name at the top of the New Show Rating Chart.

Give the schedule to a parent or grownup you live with. Ask

that person to choose a show he or she would like for you to watch and evaluate. Write the name of that show on the Parent's Choice Rating Chart.

Because you will be watching all four shows this week, be sure that no two are scheduled at the same time.

Step 6 Rating Your Programs

Keep your rating charts with you as you watch the four programs you will evaluate. When a program is over, rate how well it did for each quality on your chart. Then circle a number, using the key at the bottom of the charts to guide you.

To get an overall rating, add the four rating numbers together. Then divide that total by 4 because you rated four qualities. The answer is your overall rating. Write it in the box at the bottom of the chart. If you have trouble with division, ask a parent for help or use a calculator.

Good Show Rating Chart

Example: Amy Chose "M.A.S.H." as her good show. The episode she watched was not as funny as some. Still, she found it interesting to watch. As she watched, she noticed that

Program _____ M.A.S.H._____

Qualities	Ratings
funny	1 2 ③ 4 5
likeable characters	1 2 3 4 ⑤
surprising	1 2 3 ④ 5
leaves me happy	1 2 3 ④ 5
Overall rating	⑯ ÷ 4 = 4

the people on "M.A.S.H." seemed like her friends. She did not think of them as actors playing parts. See the chart above for her ratings of "M.A.S.H."

Amy figured out her overall rating by adding the four number ratings together. She wrote this number in the circle at the bottom of the chart. Then she divided the total by 4 and wrote the answer in the box. This was her overall rating.

MASTERING MULTIPLICATION

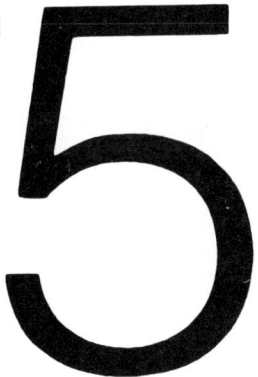

Scope

Five week-long assignments.

1. Seeing Double
2. The Fives Facts
3. The No-Sweat Nines
4. The Perfect Squares
5. The Last Facts

Additional Classroom Uses

Math ■ playing student-created math games
■ sharing multiplication tricks

Study Skills ■ working in pairs to master multiplication

Curriculum Integration

Math ■ adding equal sets (multiplication) ■ learning multiplication facts ■ finding patterns ■ learning the commutative property ■ completing a matrix (multiplication table) ■ squaring numbers ■ understanding multiplication symbols

Language ■ interviewing ■ teaching multiplication tricks
■ teaching math games

Study Skills ■ creating math games
■ making and using flash cards ■ discovering memory aids

Challenges for GATE Students

■ finding patterns ■ creating computer drills
■ applying learning modalities ■ helping less able students
■ applying concepts of money and time

Unit Five

Dear Parent(s):

It is time for your child to learn multiplication. Over the next few weeks he or she will be bringing home assignments that reinforce what we will be doing in class in math.

You may be surprised to find that we will not begin with the ones and march doggedly onward through the nines. Instead we will start with the twos, which the children already know whenever they add a number to itself such as 3 + 3 or 8 + 8. From there we shift to the fives, which most children are familiar with from handling money. At that point we tackle the nines, having found from experience that once children have mastered their nines they usually feel they can handle anything.

You can assist your child in several ways throughout these assignments. In each assignment he or she will be filling out multiplication tables and then transferring this information to a Mastering Multiplication Chart that has all the tables from 0 to 9. You can help by making certain that the facts on the tables and the chart are correct. You can also make life easier for both of you by encouraging your child to keep the Mastering Multiplication Chart in a safe place, because it will be needed over the next few weeks. In addition, you may find yourself counting toothpicks, learning to multiply on your fingers, playing multiplication games, and helping with good old-fashioned drill.

My hope is that these homework assignments will help make learning multiplication more interesting and less intimidating than it was for many of us. Nothing, however, will completely eliminate the necessity of drill for some students. I suggest you keep your child's Mastering Multiplication Chart around your home and use it for drill if your child has difficulty remembering all the multiplication facts. Your interest and assistance can help make the difference between success and frustration for your child in multiplication.

Sincerely,

Mastering Multiplication

I. Preassessment Considerations

A. This unit is designed to be used with all third-grade students who are beginning to learn multiplication. It will also be useful for fourth graders who need to review their multiplication facts after a summer of forgetfulness. You might also use these assignments with second graders gifted in math who can't wait to get on with multiplication.

B. The assignments can be used in any order as long as the first and last assignments remain in their present sequence. The order of these assignments, however, has been carefully thought out and tested with students. The rationale for this approach is as follows.

1. The twos are first introduced in "Seeing Double." The twos are an easy place to begin, because children already know these facts from addition. This assignment concentrates on the concept of multiplication.

2. The fives are covered next in "The Fives Facts." Most students find this jump an easy one, because they are used to counting by fives both from telling time and handling money. Multiplying by fives feels easy and natural.

3. The next jump is to the nines in "The No-Sweat Nines." This assignment is a great confidence booster. Before sending this assignment home, you should teach your students finger multiplication to make the nines easy. This trick is illustrated in the student assignment sheets. Once they master these facts they are ready for anything.

4. The fourth assignment, "The Perfect Squares," takes a different approach, teaching only the squares from one to nine. Children learn the concept of squaring a number in a natural way while learning new facts and reviewing others they already know.

5. In the final assignment, "The Last Facts," students are encouraged to analyze and apply patterns to finish learning the zeros and ones. They are then ready to learn the remaining facts by playing a variety of last-facts games.

C. Each of these assignments can be done in one week. Students should track their progress from assignment to assignment by filling in their Mastering Multiplication Charts. By the time students finish "The Last Facts," this chart should be complete.

II. Integration into the Classroom

(*Note:* Because these assignments are concerned with the same basic material, these suggestions are designed to be used with the entire unit.)

A. **Classroom Multiplication Chart.** Post a large version of the Mastering Multiplication Chart in your classroom. Fill in the chart as students work through the assignments. This process will reinforce what students have done individually and will give them a model against which to check their own charts. As the chart begins to fill out, you will all feel a satisfying sense of progress.

B. **Working with Partners.** Throughout these assignments, student interest and motivation will be enhanced if children work with partners. You might pair students in many ways, including responsible with scatterbrained, highly organized with creative, math lover with math hater, and visual learner with auditory learner. However you group students, emphasize that they are all responsible not only for their own progress, but also for that of their partners. Besides drilling each other on the facts learned so far, partners can work together on these activities:

1. Seeing Double. Repeat steps 1 and 2 in class as a team, using 10 sheets of paper and manipulatives that you provide or that students bring from home. Some children will enjoy this activity more if they use their own pennies, seashells, or pebbles.
2. The Fives Facts. Ask each pair to make a paper clock, and then challenge them to find a way to use the clock to help them remember the fives.
3. The No-Sweat Nines. Partners should compare notes on nines tricks they learned at home and teach each other what they have learned. Then they might teach other pairs.
4. The Perfect Squares. Team partners into groups of four to play each student's Perfect Square Game.
5. The Last Facts. With their partners students should play at least one of the last-facts games in step 5. Any children bringing in new games should play them first with their regular partners.

C. **Collecting Multiplication Games.** Place any multiplication games created by students in a mini-learning center to be played in students' free time. If a game is not self-evident, ask the creator to write down rules or instructions.

III. Activities for GATE Students

A. **Finding Multiplication Patterns.** Show your GATE students how to make a multiplication table for 0 through 11, and have them fill it out. Then challenge them to find patterns in the table. They already know the fives pattern. What others can they spot? For example, all numbers multiplied by 10 end in 0, and all numbers from 1 to 9 multiplied by 11 are doubles of themselves.

x	0	1	2	3	4	5	6	7	8	9	10	11
0												
1												
2												
3												
4												
5												
6												
7												
8												
9												
10												
11												

B. **Creating Computer Drills.** If your class has access to a computer, challenge a novice programmer to create a drill program for each week's new facts. Before having other students use the program, check it yourself for any bugs.

C. **Applying Learning Modalities.** Students who have completed "Learning to Learn Spelling Words" should be able to create a variety of learning activities to help children learn their multiplication facts. Be sure the activities emphasize different learning modalities. Then have students try out their activities with those having trouble remembering their times tables.

Name

Date Due
Page 1 of 4

Seeing Double

Learning to multiply by 2 is easy. Try it for yourself.

Skills you will develop

- writing multiplication facts
- multiplying by 2

What you will need

- pencil
- 10 sheets of blank paper
- 100 small objects
- Mastering Multiplication Chart

Before you begin: Find 100 toothpicks, pennies, pebbles, beans, or other small objects. All 100 objects should be the same item.

Using Objects to Make Doubles

Multiplying by 2 is easy. Think of it as doubles when you roll a pair of dice.

  2 × 3

Double 3s are the same as 2 groups of 3.

  2 × 6

Double 6s are the same as 2 groups of 6.

 • 2 × 1

Double 1s, or snake eyes, are the same as 2 groups of 1.

This week you will be learning your twos multiplication facts. To begin, get 10 sheets of blank paper. Fold each of them in half the long way. Write the letter *A* at the top of the left side of each sheet. Write the letter *B* at the top of the right side of each sheet.

Spread out all 10 sheets on a table or on the floor.

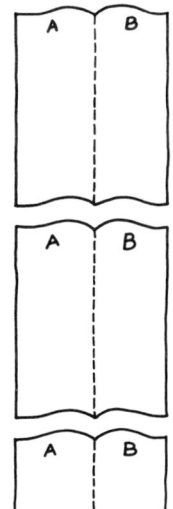

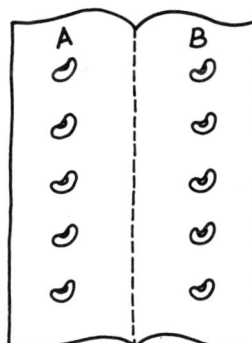 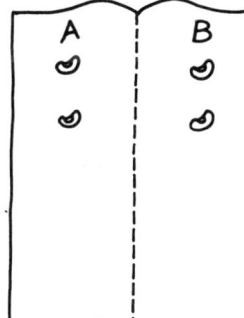 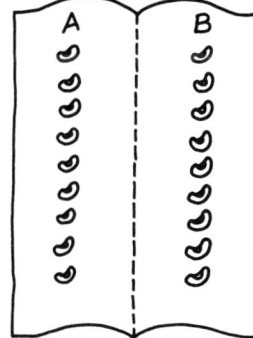

Unit Five

77

Start with the closest sheet of paper. Put any number of objects from 0 to 9 in the *A* space. Put the same number in the *B* space of the same sheet.

Do the same thing for each sheet of paper using another number each time. When you are finished, you should have double groups of 0, 1, 2, 3, 4, 5, 6, 7, 8, and 9.

Stop here until you can find a grownup to look at your sheets. Ask these questions.

- Does each sheet show doubles? Is the *A* group the same size as the *B* group on each sheet?
- Which sheet shows double 1s?
- Which sheet shows double 0s?

Next, tell the grownup an addition fact for each sheet.

Example: 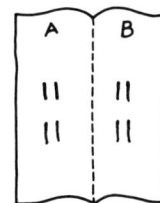   Addition fact

$4 + 4 = 8$

Leave your sheets out until you have completed step 3.

Learning to Write Multiplication Facts

Here is a multiplication fact.

$$2 \times 4 = 8$$

This is the same as saying 2 groups of 4 equal 8. Fill in the blanks in these multiplication facts.

2 groups of 7 equal 14

☐ × ☐ = 14

2 groups of 1 equal 2

2 × ☐ = ☐

2 groups of 9 equal 18

☐ × ☐ = ☐

2 groups of 2 equal 4

Step 3: Writing Multiplication Facts

Look at one of your sheets. What multiplication fact is shown there? Write it at the bottom of the page. Do the same for the other sheets.

Examples:

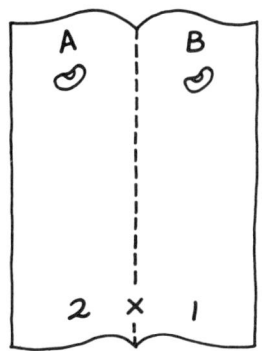
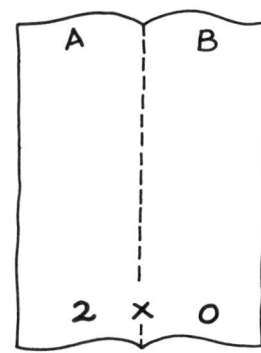

When you have finished, ask your grownup to check each fact. When they are all correct, use the facts to fill in this twos table.

Twos Table

$2 \times 0 =$	
$2 \times 1 =$	
$2 \times 2 =$	
$2 \times 3 =$	
$2 \times 4 =$	
$2 \times 5 =$	
$2 \times 6 =$	
$2 \times 7 =$	
$2 \times 8 =$	
$2 \times 9 =$	

Step 4: Practicing the Twos

Use your multiplication facts to do these problems.

$2 \times 6 =$ ☐ $2 \times 0 =$ ☐ $2 \times 3 =$ ☐

$2 \times 5 =$ ☐ $2 \times 9 =$ ☐ $2 \times 4 =$ ☐

$2 \times 7 =$ ☐ $2 \times 2 =$ ☐ $2 \times 8 =$ ☐

$2 \times 1 =$ ☐

$$\begin{array}{r} 3 \\ \times\ 2 \\ \hline \end{array} \quad \begin{array}{r} 1 \\ \times\ 2 \\ \hline \end{array} \quad \begin{array}{r} 7 \\ \times\ 2 \\ \hline \end{array} \quad \begin{array}{r} 9 \\ \times\ 2 \\ \hline \end{array} \quad \begin{array}{r} 4 \\ \times\ 2 \\ \hline \end{array}$$

$$\begin{array}{r} 2 \\ \times\ 2 \\ \hline \end{array} \quad \begin{array}{r} 5 \\ \times\ 2 \\ \hline \end{array} \quad \begin{array}{r} 8 \\ \times\ 2 \\ \hline \end{array} \quad \begin{array}{r} 6 \\ \times\ 2 \\ \hline \end{array} \quad \begin{array}{r} 0 \\ \times\ 2 \\ \hline \end{array}$$

Unit Five — Seeing Double

 ## Turning the Twos Around

Is 2 × 6 the same as 6 × 2? Find out for yourself. Here are 2 groups of 6. Count them and complete the multiplication fact.

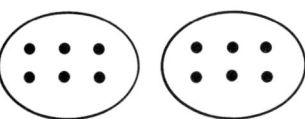 2 × 6 = ☐

Here are 6 groups of 2. Count them and complete the multiplication fact.

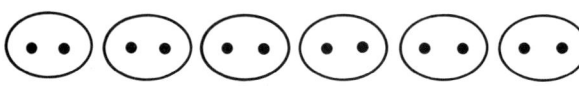 6 × 2 = ☐

You have learned more than you think. Turn the rest of the twos facts around. You have also begun to learn the zeros through the nines. Fill in those facts here.

0 × 2 = ☐   4 × 2 = ☐   7 × 2 = ☐

1 × 2 = ☐   5 × 2 = ☐   8 × 2 = ☐

3 × 2 = ☐   6 × 2 = ☐   9 × 2 = ☐

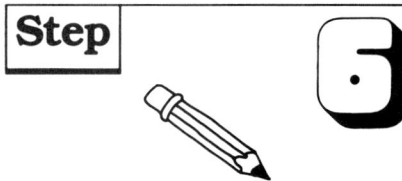 ## Beginning Your Mastering Multiplication Chart

You are ready to begin filling in your Mastering Multiplication Chart. Begin with the twos table. Fill it in completely.

Next, fill in the facts you learned in step 5. You should have one fact filled in in each of the other tables.

Example: 7 × 2 = 14

Sevens Table

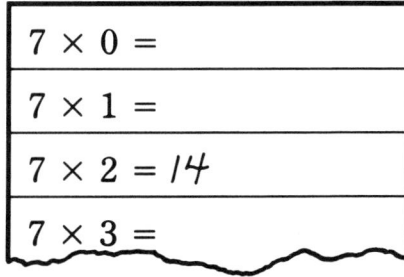

Mastering Multiplication Chart

Name: _____

Date Due: _____

Keep this chart in a safe place for the next few weeks.

Page 1 of 2

Zeros Table

$0 \times 0 =$
$0 \times 1 =$
$0 \times 2 =$
$0 \times 3 =$
$0 \times 4 =$
$0 \times 5 =$
$0 \times 6 =$
$0 \times 7 =$
$0 \times 8 =$
$0 \times 9 =$

Ones Table

$1 \times 0 =$
$1 \times 1 =$
$1 \times 2 =$
$1 \times 3 =$
$1 \times 4 =$
$1 \times 5 =$
$1 \times 6 =$
$1 \times 7 =$
$1 \times 8 =$
$1 \times 9 =$

Twos Table

$2 \times 0 =$
$2 \times 1 =$
$2 \times 2 =$
$2 \times 3 =$
$2 \times 4 =$
$2 \times 5 =$
$2 \times 6 =$
$2 \times 7 =$
$2 \times 8 =$
$2 \times 9 =$

Threes Table

$3 \times 0 =$
$3 \times 1 =$
$3 \times 2 =$
$3 \times 3 =$
$3 \times 4 =$
$3 \times 5 =$
$3 \times 6 =$
$3 \times 7 =$
$3 \times 8 =$
$3 \times 9 =$

Fours Table

$4 \times 0 =$
$4 \times 1 =$
$4 \times 2 =$
$4 \times 3 =$
$4 \times 4 =$
$4 \times 5 =$
$4 \times 6 =$
$4 \times 7 =$
$4 \times 8 =$
$4 \times 9 =$

Unit Five

Mastering Multiplication Chart

Fives Table

5 × 0 =
5 × 1 =
5 × 2 =
5 × 3 =
5 × 4 =
5 × 5 =
5 × 6 =
5 × 7 =
5 × 8 =
5 × 9 =

Sixes Table

6 × 0 =
6 × 1 =
6 × 2 =
6 × 3 =
6 × 4 =
6 × 5 =
6 × 6 =
6 × 7 =
6 × 8 =
6 × 9 =

Sevens Table

7 × 0 =
7 × 1 =
7 × 2 =
7 × 3 =
7 × 4 =
7 × 5 =
7 × 6 =
7 × 7 =
7 × 8 =
7 × 9 =

Eights Table

8 × 0 =
8 × 1 =
8 × 2 =
8 × 3 =
8 × 4 =
8 × 5 =
8 × 6 =
8 × 7 =
8 × 8 =
8 × 9 =

Nines Table

9 × 0 =
9 × 1 =
9 × 2 =
9 × 3 =
9 × 4 =
9 × 5 =
9 × 6 =
9 × 7 =
8 × 8 =
9 × 9 =

Name

Date Due

The Fives Facts

If you can count by 5s, you can learn to multiply by 5.

Skills you will develop
- finding patterns
- multiplying by 5

What you will need
- pencil
- 9 nickels
- Mastering Multiplication Chart

Before you begin: Raid your piggy bank, pockets, coin collection, or sugar jar for nine nickels. If you can't find that many, find at least one. You can use it over and over again.

Step 1

Finding the Fives Facts

Are you like Donald Duck's rich Uncle Scrooge? Do you enjoy handling coins and counting them? If you do, learning to multiply by 5 will be fun.

Gather your nickels. A nickel is worth 5 cents or 5 pennies. When you want to know how much a bunch of nickels is worth, you count by 5s. How much is 5 nickels worth?

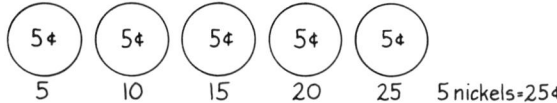

Use your nickels to find out the fives facts. Look at the fives facts chart on the next page. It begins with the fact 1 × 5 = _____. Put one nickel in the first box beside that fact. Trace around the nickel with your pencil. Then complete the fact by counting by 5s. Do the same for the rest of the fives facts there. Here are two examples.

Five piles of five pennies is the same as five nickels. 5 × 5 = 25

Unit Five

$2 \times 5 =$	$4 \times 5 =$						
$1 \times 5 =$	$3 \times 5 =$	$5 \times 5 =$	$6 \times 5 =$	$7 \times 5 =$	$8 \times 5 =$	$9 \times 5 =$

The Fives Facts

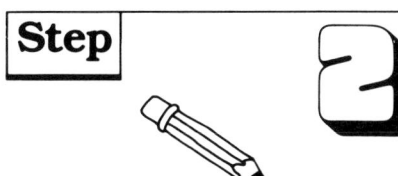

Turning the Fives Around

Is 3 × 5 the same as 5 × 3? Here are 3 groups of 5. Count the dots and fill in the multiplication fact.

Hint: Think of 5 × 0 as having no nickels at all.

Fives Table

 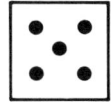 

3 × 5 = _____

Here are 5 groups of 3. Count the dots and finish the fact.

   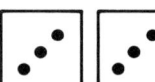

5 × 3 = _____

5 × 0 =
5 × 1 =
5 × 2 =
5 × 3 =
5 × 4 =
5 × 5 =
5 × 6 =
5 × 7 =
5 × 8 =
5 × 9 =

Turn the rest of your fives facts around and fill in this fives table.

Ask someone who knows how to multiply to check your table before you go on.

Finding Patterns

Can you spot the pattern in your fives table? Look at the last numeral in each of your facts. In the fact 5 × 9 = 45, for example, the last numeral is 5. What do you notice about the last numeral of all your facts?

_____

Look again and then complete this pattern description.

When 5 is multiplied by an even number like 2 or 4, the answer ends with the numeral _____.

When 5 is multiplied by an odd number such as 3 or 7, the answer ends with the numeral _____.

Step 4 — Practicing the Fives

$$\begin{array}{cccccccc}
3 & 1 & 7 & 6 & 4 & 0 & 8 & 2 \\
\times 5 & \times 5 & \times 5 & \times 5 & \times 5 & \times 5 & \times 5 & \times 5 \\
\hline
\end{array}$$

5 × 5 = _____   5 × 9 = _____   8 × 5 = _____

3 × 5 = _____   1 × 5 = _____

$$\begin{array}{ccccccccc}
5 & 5 & 5 & 5 & 5 & 5 & 9 & 5 \\
\times 5 & \times 6 & \times 9 & \times 4 & \times 7 & \times 0 & \times 5 & \times 2 \\
\hline
\end{array}$$

5 × 8 = _____   6 × 5 = _____   5 × 3 = _____

7 × 5 = _____   4 × 5 = _____

Step 5 — Continuing Your Mastering Multiplication Chart

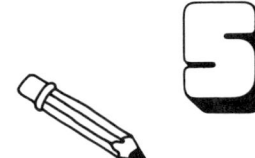

Fill in the fives table on your Mastering Multiplication Chart. Then fill in the facts you found in step 1.

Your twos and fives tables should be complete now. You should also have two facts complete in the rest of your tables. Here, for example, is how your threes table should look.

Threes Table

3 × 0 =
3 × 1 =
3 × 2 = 6
3 × 3 =
3 × 4 =
3 × 5 = 15
3 × 6 =

Name

Date Due

The No-Sweat Nines

Let your fingers do the multiplying as you learn your nines.

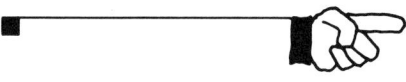

Skills you will develop

- multiplying by 9
- teaching a skill

What you will need

- pencil
- marking pen
- 3 people who are older than you
- Mastering Multiplication Chart

Before you begin: You should have learned the nines finger multiplication trick in class. If you missed this lesson, ask your teacher to show you how it works.

Reviewing Finger Multiplication

Take a moment to review the finger multiplication trick you learned in class. You may want to begin by using a marking pen to number your fingernails.

Try multiplying 9 × 8. Bend down the finger marked 8. Count the fingers to the left of your bent finger to get the tens.

_____.

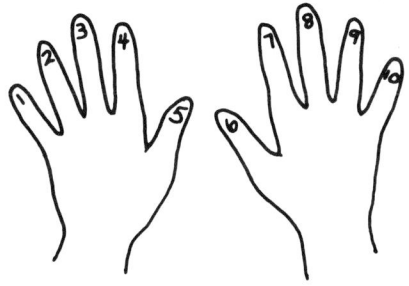

Count the fingers to the right of your bent finger to get the ones.

_____.

so 9 × 8 = 72

Complete this fact:

9 × 8 = ☐

Use your fingers to fill in all the facts in the nines table. There is one fact that cannot be shown on your fingers.

9 × 0 = 0

Nines Table

9 × 0 =	
9 × 1 =	
9 × 2 =	
9 × 3 =	
9 × 4 =	
9 × 5 =	
9 × 6 =	
9 × 7 =	
9 × 8 =	
9 × 9 =	

Unit Five

Step 2

Teaching Finger Multiplication

Sit down with someone older than you who knows multiplication. Ask that person to check over your nines table. Be sure all your facts are correct.

Next, teach that person the nines finger multiplication trick. Then ask the questions in this box, and record that person's answers. Do the same with two other people.

First person's name:_____
Do you like this nines trick?_____
Can you show me another trick for multiplying by 9?____ (If the answer is yes, learn that trick and bring it to class.)

Second person's name:_____
Do you like this nines trick?_____
Can you show me another trick for multiplying by 9?____ (If the answer is yes, learn that trick and bring it to class.)

Third person's name:_____
Do you like this nines trick?_____
Can you show me another trick for multiplying by 9?____ (If the answer is yes, learn that trick and bring it to class.)

The No-Sweat Nines

Step 3: Practicing the Nines

Use your fingers only when you get stuck.

9 × 4 = _____   9 × 8 = _____   9 × 5 = _____

9 × 6 = _____   9 × 3 = _____   9 × 7 = _____

9 × 9 = _____   9 × 2 = _____

$\begin{array}{r} 1 \\ \times\ 9 \\ \hline \end{array}$ $\begin{array}{r} 7 \\ \times\ 9 \\ \hline \end{array}$ $\begin{array}{r} 3 \\ \times\ 9 \\ \hline \end{array}$ $\begin{array}{r} 6 \\ \times\ 9 \\ \hline \end{array}$ $\begin{array}{r} 0 \\ \times\ 9 \\ \hline \end{array}$

$\begin{array}{r} 8 \\ \times\ 9 \\ \hline \end{array}$ $\begin{array}{r} 9 \\ \times\ 9 \\ \hline \end{array}$ $\begin{array}{r} 4 \\ \times\ 9 \\ \hline \end{array}$

Step 4: Turning the Nines Around

Turn the nines around and complete these facts.

0 × 9 = _____   5 × 9 = _____

1 × 9 = _____   6 × 9 = _____

2 × 9 = _____   7 × 9 = _____

3 × 9 = _____   8 × 9 = _____

4 × 9 = _____   9 × 9 = _____

Step 5: Continuing Your Mastering Multiplication Chart

Fill in the nines table. Then add the facts in step 4 to your other tables.

assignment sheets, any nine tricks you learned — Bring Back

Name: _____

Date Due: _____

The Perfect Squares

You can make learning the perfect squares fun by creating a math game.

Skills you will develop

- multiplying a number by itself
- creating a math game

What you will need

- pencil
- scissors
- glue or tape
- 3 sheets of blank paper
- materials for a math game
- Mastering Multiplication Chart

Step 1

Multiplying a Number by Itself

What do you notice about these multiplication facts?

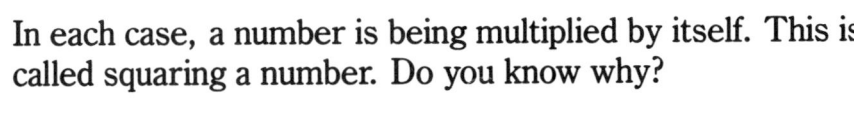

$1 \times 1 = 1 \quad 2 \times 2 = 4 \quad 5 \times 5 = 25 \quad 9 \times 9 = 81$

In each case, a number is being multiplied by itself. This is called squaring a number. Do you know why?

To find out, get your graph paper and scissors. Let's begin with the fact $2 \times 2 = 4$. To show this fact with graph paper, cut out two strips with two boxes on each strip.

Arrange those two strips to form a square. Glue or tape your perfect square on one of your blank pieces of paper.

Now use your graph paper to show the fact $3 \times 3 = 9$. Cut out three strips with three boxes on each strip. Can you find a way to arrange these three strips to form a perfect square?

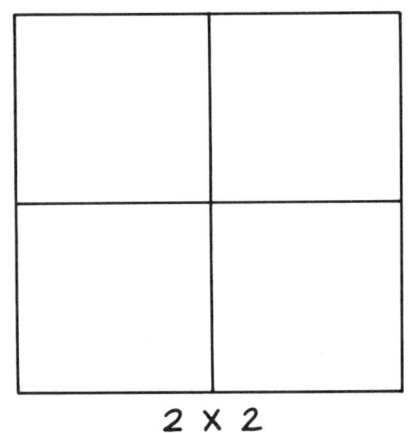

2 X 2

Cut out perfect squares from your graph paper for the facts $1 \times 1 = 1$ to $9 \times 9 = 81$. Glue or tape your squares to your blank sheets of paper. Under each perfect square, write the multiplication fact it shows. When you are finished you should have nine squares and multiplication facts. If you can't figure out how to do this, try one of these suggestions.

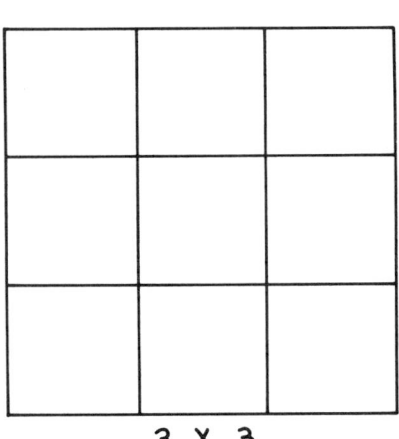

3 X 3

a. Throw a temper tantrum.
b. Call a friend for help.
c. Ask a parent for ideas.
d. Complain to your teacher tomorrow.

Step 2: Writing a Perfect Squares Table

Use the perfect square facts you learned in step 1 to fill out this table of perfect squares. The first and last facts are partly done for you.

Before going on, ask someone who knows multiplication to check your facts. Make sure that they are all correct.

Perfect Squares Table

1 x 1 =
9 x 9 =

Step 3: Creating a Perfect Squares Game

There is no special trick for remembering the perfect squares. You simply have to practice them until you can remember them. To make this practice more fun, create a game using the perfect squares. Here are some ideas to get you started.

Jump rope game: Chant a fact while you skip rope. For example, use 3 × 3 = ☐. Then try to jump exactly nine times without missing. The game gets harder with some of the other facts. Practice them all.

The Perfect Squares

Ball or balloon game: State your fact. For example, use 5 × 5 = 25. Now try to bounce your ball or hit your balloon in the air 25 times without missing. What happens when you do miss?

Clapping-chanting game: Sit in a circle with two or three other people. Start a clapping pattern. The first person chants, "One times one equals one." Without breaking the pattern, the second person chants, "Two times two equals four." You will have to decide what happens when someone makes a mistake or can't remember the next perfect square.

Board game: Make up a board game. Each of the playing spaces should have one of the numerals 1 through 9 in it. When a player lands on a space, he or she must say the perfect square multiplication fact for the number there. If the space has the number 8 in it, the player must say, "eight times eight equals sixty-four." You will have to decide what happens if a player doesn't know that fact.

Practicing the Perfect Squares

After playing your game, this practice should be easy.

$$\begin{array}{r}5\\ \times\,5\\ \hline\end{array}\qquad\begin{array}{r}7\\ \times\,7\\ \hline\end{array}\qquad\begin{array}{r}3\\ \times\,3\\ \hline\end{array}\qquad\begin{array}{r}6\\ \times\,6\\ \hline\end{array}\qquad\begin{array}{r}2\\ \times\,2\\ \hline\end{array}$$

$$\begin{array}{r}4\\ \times\,4\\ \hline\end{array}\qquad\begin{array}{r}9\\ \times\,9\\ \hline\end{array}\qquad\begin{array}{r}1\\ \times\,1\\ \hline\end{array}\qquad\begin{array}{r}8\\ \times\,8\\ \hline\end{array}$$

Continuing Your Mastering Multiplication Chart

Add all the perfect squares to your Mastering Multiplication Chart. You will find that some of them are already there.

Name _____

Date Due
Page 1 of 5

The Last Facts

You are almost finished learning your multiplication facts. Was it as hard as you thought it would be?

Skills you will develop
- finding patterns
- multiplying by 0, 1, 3, 4, 6, 7, 8

What you will need
- pencil
- scissors
- heavy paper

Step 1

Multiplying by 0

You are ready now to finish learning the last facts on your Mastering Multiplication Chart. Get out your chart and a pencil.

Look at the zeros table. What pattern do you see in the facts already completed? Use that pattern to fill out the rest of the table.

Turn those facts around. Fill in the first fact in the other tables that are not yet completed. In the fours table, for example, that fact will be $4 \times 0 =$ _____.

Fours Table

First fact →	$4 \times 0 =$
Second fact →	$4 \times 1 =$
	$4 \times 2 = 8$

Step 2

Multiplying by 1

Study the ones table on your chart. You should be able to find the pattern in the facts already completed. Use that pattern to fill in the rest of that table.

Turn those facts around. Fill in the second fact in the other tables that are not complete.

If you have any doubts about your zeros and ones tables, ask someone who knows multiplication to check them for you.

Step 3

Matching Multiplication Facts

Here are the last 20 facts you need to learn. The facts in the left column are complete. Those in the right column are not. Turn each fact on the left around. Match it to a fact on the right. Then complete the matching fact. The first one has been matched and completed for you.

The Last 20 Facts

3 × 4 = 12	8 × 7 = _____
3 × 6 = 18	8 × 6 = _____
3 × 7 = 21	8 × 4 = _____
3 × 8 = 24	8 × 3 = _____
4 × 6 = 24	7 × 6 = _____
4 × 7 = 28	7 × 4 = _____
4 × 8 = 32	7 × 3 = _____
6 × 7 = 42	6 × 4 = _____
6 × 8 = 48	6 × 3 = _____
7 × 8 = 56	4 × 3 = _____

You can see that if you learn the 10 facts on the right, you will also know the 10 on the left.

Step 4

Creating Last-Facts Cards

There is no trick for learning these last facts. You will have to repeat them over and over until you remember them. You can make this job easier by playing several last-facts card games.

To make your last-facts cards you need some heavy paper. Construction paper, lightweight cardboard, or old grocery bags will work. Cut out 21 cards using the pattern on page 96.

Write the last 20 multiplication facts from step 3 on your cards. Use a ☐ instead of the product (answer). Draw your own picture of the Joker on the extra card.

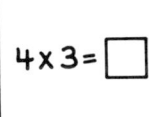

Step 5

Playing Last-Fact Games

Use your last-fact cards to play these games.

Concentration 1 or 2 players

Lay your last-facts cards face down on a table. Turn over two cards. Say each fact on the cards and the product (answer) aloud. If the two cards match, such as $4 \times 6 = \square$ and $6 \times 4 = \square$, keep them. If they don't, turn them down again.

Keep turning over pairs of cards until you have matched them all. Don't forget to say the fact and product out loud every time you turn over a card.

Fish 2 or 3 players

Deal out four cards to each player. To "fish" for a card to match one in your hand, say something like this: "I have 6×8. I am fishing for 48. Does anyone have it?"

Your fishing isn't legal unless you tell what fact you have and what product (answer) you want. If no one has the card you want, draw from the pile. If you do get your match, fish again.

Joker 2 or 3 players

Deal out all the cards, including the "joker." On your turn, draw a card from the hand of the player to your left. If that card matches one in your hand, lay both cards in front of you. For each card, say both the fact and product (answer) out loud for the other players. Keep playing until all the cards are matched and someone is stuck with the joker.

War 2 players

Divide your last-facts cards into two equal piles. The first player turns over a card and says the product (answer). The second player does the same thing. The person with the highest product wins both cards. If one person has $3 \times 8 = \square$ and the other has $7 \times 8 = \square$, the second player wins the cards. In case of a tie, turn over two more cards and do it again.

Card Pattern
Cut this out and trace around it to make your cards.

The game is over when one person has all the cards. Remember to say each product (answer) aloud whenever you turn up another card.

Your Own Game

Find another way to use your last-facts cards. Can you think of another card game? Or can you use your cards as part of a board game you like?

If you come up with a good idea, bring it to class to share with your friends.

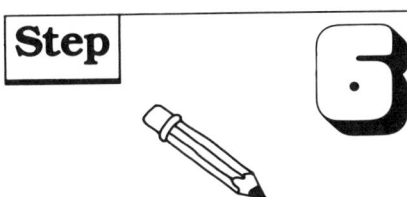

Practicing the Last Facts

After playing your games, these problems shouldn't be too hard.

$$\begin{array}{cccccc} 0 & 7 & 9 & 3 & 4 & 7 \\ \times 5 & \times 4 & \times 1 & \times 6 & \times 3 & \times 0 \end{array}$$

$$\begin{array}{cccccc} 1 & 6 & 1 & 8 & 0 & 4 \\ \times 1 & \times 8 & \times 3 & \times 7 & \times 1 & \times 8 \end{array}$$

$$\begin{array}{cccccc} 8 & 2 & 1 & 3 & 6 & 9 \\ \times 3 & \times 0 & \times 5 & \times 4 & \times 4 & \times 0 \end{array}$$

$$\begin{array}{cccccc} 2 & 8 & 4 & 1 & 7 & 6 \\ \times 1 & \times 6 & \times 7 & \times 6 & \times 1 & \times 3 \end{array}$$

$$\begin{array}{cccccc} 3 & 7 & 0 & 8 & 7 & 3 \\ \times 8 & \times 3 & \times 3 & \times 4 & \times 6 & \times 7 \end{array}$$

$$\begin{array}{cccccc} 1 & 7 & 4 & 4 & 6 & 0 \\ \times 8 & \times 8 & \times 6 & \times 0 & \times 7 & \times 8 \end{array}$$

If you had trouble with some of these problems, use your last-facts cards for extra practice. Give a friend or parent your cards. Have that person ask you the first part of each fact, such as 7 × 4 =. If you can't remember the rest of that fact, look at the card. Then put it in a pile of facts you need to work on. Go through the cards again and again until you remember all the facts.

Step  **Completing Your Mastering Multiplication Chart**

Use your last-facts cards to finish filling in your Mastering Multiplication Chart. If you find you left out some other facts, fill them in now.

Congratulations! You have finished learning your multiplication facts. Use your chart to review them often. If you find you have forgotten some facts, write them on cards and have a friend help you practice.

I, _____, am hereby awarded the title of MULTIPLICATION MASTER

assignment sheets, last-fact cards, games to share

Bring Back

COMMUNITIES

Scope

Five week-long assignments. Some assignments may overlap others. The first four may be used with all students. The final assignment might be done in small groups led by GATE students.

1. Plant and Animal Communities
2. Grandparents' Communities
3. A Parent's Community
4. My Own Community
5. Bike Town—Planning a Community

Additional Classroom Uses

Social Studies ■ collecting, analyzing, and synthesizing information ■ doing map activities ■ comparing past and present communities

Language ■ clustering information ■ writing comparison paragraphs ■ writing letters

Science ■ exploring nature's balance ■ predicting change ■ understanding cause and effect

Fine Arts ■ discussing elements of design ■ illustrating

Curriculum Integration

Math ■ estimating animal populations

Social Studies ■ working in committees ■ gathering information about past and present communities ■ community planning

Oral Language ■ eliciting feedback ■ interviewing ■ making a presentation

Written Language ■ writing letters ■ summarizing

Science ■ selecting a plant or animal community ■ identifying plants and animals ■ categorizing animals ■ making hypotheses

Fine Arts ■ creating a presentation ■ designing a poster ■ representing a planned community

Challenges for GATE Students

■ creating plant and animal communities ■ synthesizing
■ hypothesizing ■ analyzing ■ communicating
■ developing leadership skills ■ researching
■ computer programming ■ map building
■ planning a community tour

Unit Six

Dear Parent(s):

We are beginning a series of homework projects that center around the theme of community. Over the next few weeks your child will be observing a plant and animal community, corresponding with a grandparent about his or her childhood community, interviewing a parent about the community in which he or she grew up, and collecting information about the community you live in today. In addition, he or she may be doing some community planning for a town without automobiles.

You can assist your child most by serving as a resource person. Your help will be particularly important in the assignment "A Parent's Community." Besides interviewing a parent, your child will be creating a presentation about that parent's childhood community. He or she will need a parent's cooperation to do this. Some children may be bringing old photos, beloved childhood toys, and other souvenirs of their parents' pasts to class to share. I assure you that we will treat such treasures with the care and respect they deserve and will make every effort to get them home again safely.

In the assignment "Bike Town—Planning a Community," your child will move from the past and present to the future. The whole family might enjoy discussing what a town without automobiles could be like. Encourage everyone to let his or her imagination run wild.

Sincerely,

Plant and Animal Communities

I. Preassessment Considerations

A. Because this assignment is done outdoors, weather must be a consideration in scheduling. In most parts of the country the optimal times for studying plant and animal communities are early fall or late spring.

B. Students in urban areas may need to spend time discussing suitable places to find a community to study.

C. If safety is a concern, encourage students to use the buddy system when making observations or to limit their excursions to the schoolyard.

D. This assignment may be used with all students. Children will find that the most challenging aspects of the assignment are (1) identifying and labeling plants and animals and (2) making predictions.

II. Integration into the Classroom

A. **Mini-Field Trip.** One way to begin this assignment is to take students on a mini-field trip in the schoolyard or to a nearby planted area. You can use this time to practice identifying and estimating or to complete the first two steps of the assignment. If you do not have coat hangers to mark off communities, use loops of string. Children will enjoy doing their observations in pairs.

B. **Classroom Survey.** When the homework comes back, take a classroom survey to find out how many plants and animals of each kind your students found. Follow up with questions suggested by the results, such as "Why are there more plant eaters than predators?" Encourage children to come up with hypotheses about their findings.

C. **Plant/Animal Community Game.** Cut up one or two uncompleted observation charts and paste the pictures without labels on name tags. Make one tag for each child to wear during the game. Then give your students these directions.

   1. Category groups: Group yourselves according to the four categories you used to label your charts—plants, plant eaters, predators, and scavengers. Have students write their category on their name tags.

Category Groups

Unit Six   Plant and Animal Communities

2. **Community groups:** Regroup yourselves into four or five complete communities, making sure there are plants, plant eaters, predators, and scavengers in each group. If your community is missing some category, find another group with extras and kidnap one, or combine with another community.

Next, give each community group one of these "what if" problems to ponder for a few minutes. Then ask the groups to share their speculations with the class.

> a. What if a horde of army ants came through your community and ate every plant and animal above the ground? What would happen to the creatures living below the ground?
>
> b. What if it rained for 40 days and 40 nights? What parts of your community would suffer most? What parts would survive without harm?
>
> c. What if there were a long dry period and all the plants withered and died? What would the rest of your community do?
>
> d. What if hungry toads and lizards came through your community and ate up every predator, leaving the plant eaters alone? What would happen to the plants and plant eaters?
>
> e. What if someone sprayed all the plants in your community with a deadly pesticide that poisoned all the plant eaters? How would this change your community?

III. Extensions for GATE Students

A. Classroom Plant and Animal Communities. Have your GATE students create one or more of these communities for your classroom.

1. **Isopod community:** Begin with two transparent half-gallon plastic containers. Poke holes in the one that serves as a lid. Cover the bottom of the other with two cups of soil and add a handful of sphagnum moss, several isopods (sow and pill bugs) and two potato halves. Keep the soil moist to the touch and occasionally add more potato.

2. **Mealworm community:** Cover the bottom of a half-gallon container with bran flakes and add mealworms, which are available in pet stores. If you are lucky you will be able to get them in all stages: larvae, pupae, and adult beetles. Add two potatoes for food, and replace them as they dry out.

3. **Snail community:** Again you will need two half-gallon containers with holes poked in the one used as a top. Begin with a handful of sphagnum moss, and add snails and a fresh lettuce leaf. As each leaf wilts or is consumed, add a fresh one.

B. Invisible Scavengers Report. Ask one of your science-oriented GATE students to investigate the less visible scavengers such as fungi, mold, and bacteria. The section Making a Presentation in Unit 9 will help that student to put together a report on his or her findings.

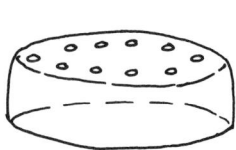 

C. **Interviewing Experts.** Ask your GATE students to find out more about a specific plant or animal community in your area by talking with an expert.

Examples: Household garden, public park, forest, stream, swamp, marsh, alpine zone, scrub lands, tidepools, prairie, baylands, grasslands, pond, desert, chaparral, vacant lot, urban forest, weed patch, farmland.

Experts might be found in any of the following places.

- garden club
- plant nursery
- aquarium
- humane society
- natural history museum
- marine biology center
- U.S. Wildlife Service
- college or university
- city parks department
- agricultural extension service
- U.S. Forest Service
- state fish and game department
- conservation organization

Before meeting with their experts, students should discuss what kinds of questions they want to ask. Afterwards they might report to the class about their interviews.

D. **Inviting Experts to Class.** If a student meets an expert who is particularly interesting and skilled at relating to children, ask that child to invite the expert to address the class. Be sure the visit is followed with a thank-you note. The sections Writing a Letter and Addressing an Envelope in Unit 9 will facilitate the letter-writing chores.

E. **Animal Community Clusters.** Some of your GATE students will enjoy learning more about animals that live in communities such as bees, beavers, fur seals, lions, hyenas, baboons, weaver birds, wasps, ants, and termites. Students can organize their findings on a Cluster Diagram from Unit 9.

F. **Wildlife Team Reports.** Team your GATE students together or with other students to do research about one of these wildlife teams.

- rhinoceroses and tick birds
- petrels and tuataras
- manta rays and remora eels
- hermit crabs and sea anemones
- crocodile birds and crocodiles
- ostriches and zebras
- aphids and ants
- long-horned beetles and scorpions
- marabou storks and griffon vultures

Student teams can be challenged to present their findings to the class in an interesting way or to write a page for a wildlife teams book.

Name

Date Due

Plant and Animal Communities

Have you ever looked closely at a weed to see what is living on it? Have you picked up a rock to see what was beneath it? You will do these things and more as you explore a small plant and animal community.

Skills you will develop

- observing
- identifying
- counting
- estimating
- recording information
- categorizing
- making predictions
- synthesizing

What you will need

- pencil
- wire coat hanger
- trowel or old spoon
- magnifying glass (useful but not necessary)
- large paper bag
- scissors
- glue or tape
- crayons or marking pens

Before you begin: Read steps 1 through 5. Bend your wire coat hanger into a rough square. Put it in your large paper bag along with your assignment sheets, pencil, trowel or spoon, and magnifying glass (if you have one). This is your observation kit.

Step

Choosing a Plant and Animal Community

People live together in communities. So do plants and animals. Like people, plants and animals that live together depend on each other to survive. Your job is to find a small plant and animal community to study. Take your observation kit with you. Here are some tips to help you pick a good spot to study.

a. It should not be too far from home or school.
b. It should have some grass or small plants. A weed patch is a perfect place to study.
c. It should be a place where people don't walk much. Many animals won't stay where there is a lot of foot traffic.

d. It should be a place where no one sprays with weed or bug killers.
e. It should be a place where no one will care if you poke around.
f. It should be a place where there is no broken glass, sharp metal, poison oak, or poison ivy to hurt you.

When you have found a good place, put your hanger on the ground. Your community will be the space *inside* the hanger.

Step 2

Making Observations in Your Community

The observation chart on pages 107–108 will help you identify and count the things living in your small community. When you find an insect inside your hanger, look at it closely. Your magnifying glass may help you. Then look at the pictures on the chart. Decide which picture looks most like your insect. Some pictures will be larger than the real insect. Make the best match you can.

Once you have identified an insect, look around the community inside your hanger for others like it. If you find just a few, count them all. Write the number you found in the space beside the insect's name on the chart. If you found six ladybugs inside your hanger, your chart would look like this.

ladybugs __6__

If you find more than 10 of your insect, don't try to count them all. Instead try to estimate or guess how many there are. One way to do this is by looking for groups of 10. In this drawing of a plant stem, the dots are aphids. These tiny insects live by sucking plant juices. Count 10 aphids and circle them with your pencil. This is your first group of 10.

Now move your eyes along the stem. When you think you have spotted about 10 more dots, change your count to 20. With the next group of about 10 you see, change your count to 30. Continue counting this way until you run out of groups of 10. How many aphids do you estimate are on the stem?

Did you see 4 groups of 10, or 40? If so, you made a good estimate. The actual number is 38. If you got 10 more or less than 40, don't worry. Estimating is a useful but difficult skill. It takes a lot of practice to become good at it.

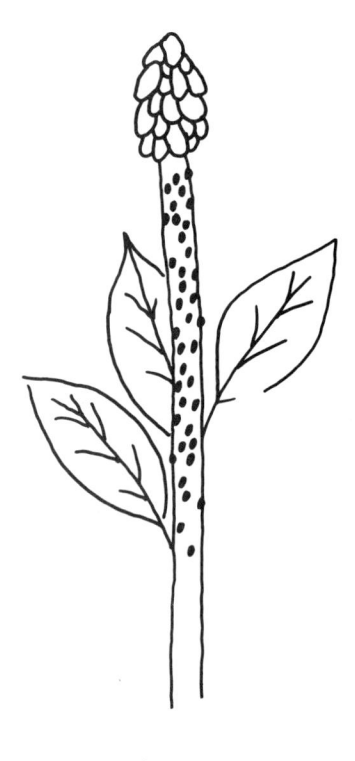

aphids_____

Plant and Animal Community Observation Chart

1. [When you get to Step 3, glue label here.]

   Look at the plants inside your hanger. How many of each kind do you see?

grass plants_____   broad leaf plants_____   mushrooms_____

2. [When you get to Step 3, glue label here.]

   Get down close to the ground to look carefully at the plants inside your hanger. Do you see any insects feeding on the leaves, stems, or flowers of the plants? Insects have six legs. Most also have wings. Many insects are caterpillars or worms before they become adults. How many of these insects can you find?

grasshoppers and crickets_____   leafhoppers_____   aphids_____   bees_____   flies_____

bugs_____   garden beetles_____   butterflies and moths_____   caterpillars and worms_____

3. [When you get to Step 3, glue label here.]

   These insects eat other insects. You may find them on the plants inside your hanger. Are any of them feeding now?

preying mantis_____   lacewings_____   ladybugs_____   wasps_____

4. When you get to Step 3, glue label here.

These animals usually hide during the day and feed on plants at night. You will find them around the bottoms of plants or under rocks and leaves.

snails_____

slugs_____

earwigs_____

5. When you get to Step 3, glue label here.

These animals might be found on plants or hiding on the ground. They eat insects or other small animals.

spiders_____

centipedes_____

salamanders_____

6. When you get to Step 3, glue label here.

These animals live by eating dead plants or dead animals. You may find some of them under rocks and pieces of wood. To find others, lay your bag out flat beside your hanger. With your trowel or spoon, dig up some dirt and put it on the bag. Then spread out the dirt to look for animals that live in the soil. Be sure to put any rocks, sticks, and dirt back in place when you are finished.

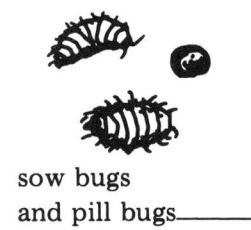
sow bugs and pill bugs_____

millipedes_____

ants_____

ground beetles_____

termites_____

worms and earthworms_____

Step  Categorizing What You Found

Read the definitions beside these labels. Then cut out the labels. Glue or tape a label beside each number on your observation chart. You will have to look carefully at your chart to know which label goes where.

| Plant Eaters |

| Plant Eaters |

Plant eaters live by feeding on parts of plants.

| Plants |

Plants are living things that are not animals. Many of them have roots and live in the ground.

| Predators |

| Predators |

Predators live by catching and eating other animals.

| Scavengers |

Scavengers live by eating dead plants or dead animals.

Step  Making Predictions

(A prediction is a guess about what will happen in the future.)

The plants, plant eaters, predators, and scavengers in your community all depend on each other. The plants provide food for the plant eaters. The plant eaters become food for predators. As plants and animals die, they are eaten by scavengers. The droppings of all these animals become part of the soil. In this way the soil gets the minerals it needs to help new plants grow.

Suppose that someone pulled up every plant inside your hanger. A few days later you go back to your hanger to repeat your observations. What predictions can you make about what would be changed? Use your observations to complete this statement.

I predict that I would not find_____

_____

_____

_____

Illustrating Your Community

Draw your plant and animal community in this space. Use your estimates on the observation chart to help you remember what plants and animals you saw and how many you saw. Try to match your colors to the colors you saw in your community.

Grandparents' Communities

I. Preassessment Considerations

A. The main activity of this assignment is writing to grandparents, which can be completed this week. The replies, however, will probably trickle in over the next two weeks. You will want to plan your follow-up activities accordingly.

B. Some children may not have a living grandparent or may not be able to call upon a grandparent for information. Suggest to these children they they write to another older relative or family friend.

C. Because writing a letter is the focus of this assignment, students who live with or live close to a grandparent should still write a letter and address an envelope, even if the end product is hand delivered.

D. If you are planning to use "My Own Community" in a couple of weeks, consider sending home the first page of that assignment now. This will give students more time to collect items for their posters.

E. This assignment will be rewarding for all your students. They will find that the most challenging parts of the assignment are writing a letter and making sure that it is mailed.

II. Integration into the Classroom

A. **Practice Letters.** Many children will not have had much experience with letter writing. You may want to discuss the four parts of a letter outlined in step 4 and have students write their first drafts in class. The assignment can then be finished at home.

B. **Mailing Letters.** Depending on the amount of confidence you have in your students, you may want to follow up to be sure that letters are mailed. Here are some ways to follow up.

   1. Have children bring their completed letters to class for you to mail.
   2. Post an "I've Mailed My Letter" list in the classroom, and have students add their names when they have mailed their letters.
   3. For students whose home resources are very limited, provide stationery, stamps, and class time for letter writing.

C. **Reading Replies.** Take time to read each reply as it comes into class. You will be surprised at the high level of interest among your students. In the discussion that follows, take time to locate on a map the community being written about, if possible.

D. **Charting Replies.** One way to represent the information in replies is to summarize it on a large chart like the following.

Grandparent's Name	Community Name/Size	Home	Main Street	School	Grocery Store	Hospital

Children should help with the task of summarizing information. As the chart fills up, look for similarities and differences depending on location, size of community, etc.

E. **Community Cluster.** Have each student fill out the following cluster diagram using the information in the grandparent's reply. Save these clusters for later comparisons with similar clusters about students' parents' communities and their own communities.

F. **Community Committees.** Divide your class into committees to gather information from grandparents' replies on one of four topics. Each committee will need to decide how it wishes to present its findings to the class. In some cases students may need to contact grandparents again for more information.

   1. Food committee: Print a book of special recipes.
      Prepare samples of one or more special dishes.
   2. Entertainment committee: Create a poster advertising a favorite entertainment such as a circus. Present an old-time entertainment such as a radio show, vaudeville act, or silent movie.
   3. Games committee: Teach the class one or more of the games mentioned in letters. Make up a book of games and rules.
   4. Celebration committee: Choose one part of a celebration to share with the class such as a square or folk dance, group sing, contest, float, rodeo act, fair judging, or pageant.

III. Extensions for GATE Students

A. **Inventions Timeline.** Have GATE students list all the inventions and modes of travel listed in grandparents' letters and then find out when each item on the list was invented or first introduced. Help students represent this information chronologically on a timeline. This timeline can also be used with information gathered in "A Parent's Community."

B. **Evaluating Inventions.** Ask students to choose the invention on the timeline that they think is most important to their lives. Stage a mini-debate in which each child defends his or her choice. Or have students write a short essay on "How My Life Would Be Different Without _____."

C. **Inventors' Biographies.** Encourage GATE students to read biographies of inventors. If you want students to share what they find out with the class, the section Making a Presentation in Unit 9 will give them guidelines for doing so in an interesting way.

IV. Adapting This Assignment to Your Classroom Program

On many occasions during the school year it may be appropriate for your students to write letters. Whether the purpose is to issue an invitation, send thanks for a special favor, gather information, offer get-well wishes, or express an opinion, the sections Writing a Letter and Addressing an Envelope in Unit 9 will help your students write their first drafts and place the elements of a letter in proper order.

Name

Date Due
Page 1 of 1

Grandparents' Community Cluster

Begin your cluster by filling in eight topics your grandparent wrote about. Then add as many details from your grandparent's letter as will fit. Topics include work, main street, climate, travel, home, celebrations, grocery store, hospital, school, games, entertainment, foods, and inventions.

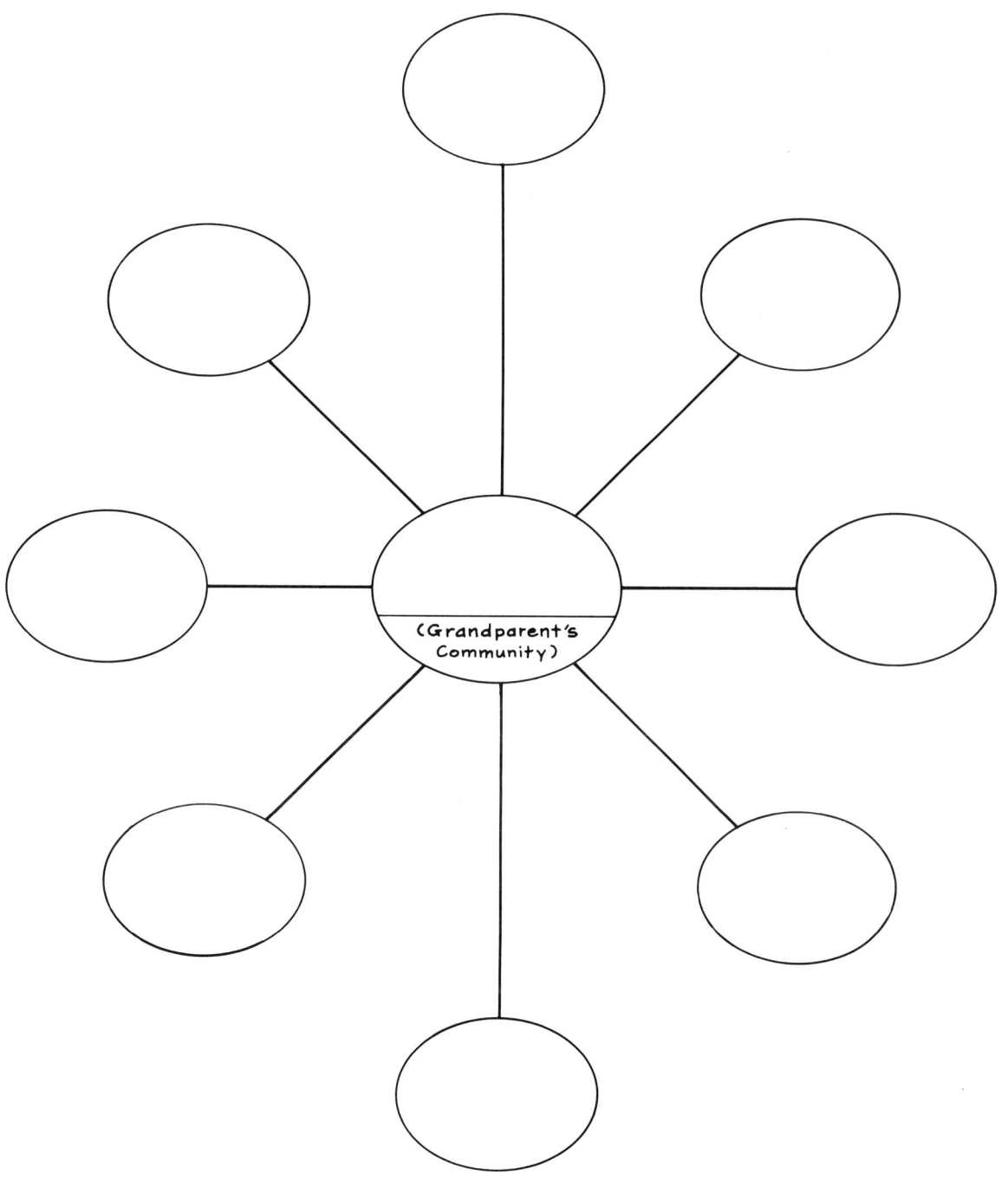

Unit Six

Grandparent's Community Cluster

Name

Date Due

Grandparents' Communities

What community did your grandparents grow up in? Was their life very different from your own? In this assignment you will find out more about a grandparent's community.

Skills you will develop

- addressing an envelope
- writing a letter
- getting feedback

What you will need

- pencil
- envelope and stamp
- writing paper

Before you begin: Read steps 1 through 4.

Step 1 Choosing Someone to Write To

This week you will write a letter to a grandparent or older friend. Your letter will include a list of questions about the community that person lived in as a child. You will find that list on the last page of this assignment.

If you are lucky, you have more than one grandparent or older friend who would enjoy hearing from you. If you have trouble choosing which person to write to, these questions may help you make up your mind.

- Which person would you like to get to know better?
- Who has lots of stories to tell about his or her childhood?
- Who likes to receive and send letters?
- Who is most likely to write back to you soon?

Once you have decided, write that person's full name and mailing address here. Ask a grownup to help you find this information.

Name_____

Street address or post office box number_____

_____

Town_____

State_____ Zip code_____

Country if person lives outside the U.S._____

Unit Six

Step 2 — Addressing an Envelope

Use the address you found in step 1 to address this envelope.

a. Your first and last name.
b. Your house number and street or post office box number.
c. Your town, state, and zip code.
d. Mr., Mrs., Miss, or Ms.
e. Person's first and last name.
f. House number and street or post office box number.
g. Name of town.
h. Name of state. Use the abbreviation if you know it.
i. Zip code.
j. Name of country if this letter is going outside the U.S.

Return address

a. _____
b. _____
c. _____

Put stamp here on real envelope.

Mailing address

d. _____ e. _____
f. _____
g. _____ h. _____ i. _____
j. _____

When you have finished, count your capital letters. Most envelopes will need at least 11. How many capitals did you use? _____

Step 3: Getting Feedback

Take out the mailing envelope you plan to use for your letter. Copy the return address and mailing address from your sample envelope in step 2 onto your real mailing envelope. Use a pencil.

When you are done, ask yourself these questions. For any *no* answers, make the needed changes on your envelope.

- Have I spelled all the names and places correctly?
- Are the house numbers or post office box numbers correct?
- Did I use the right zip code?
- Did I use capital letters to begin the names of people? streets? towns? states? countries?
- Did I put commas between the names of towns and states?
- Did I line up the person's name, address, and town correctly?
- Is my writing neat enough for workers at the post office to read?

Ask a grownup the same questions about your envelope. When all answers are *yes,* put a stamp in the right-hand corner.

Step 4: Writing a Letter

Your letter will have five parts.

Part 1: Today's date_____

Part 2: Dear_____, Fill in the name you call the person you are writing to. (Examples: Grandpa, Great Aunt Sue, Miss Hill, Charlie.)

Part 3: You might begin your letter with some news about yourself or your family. (Example: "How are you? I've been busy playing soccer after school. Last week I scored a goal.")

Part 4: The main part of your letter should explain why you are writing. (Example: "I need your help. My class is studying communities. Could you answer some of the questions on this sheet with my letter? Please mail back your answers as soon as you can. Thank you for helping me.")

Part 5: Your closing_____. If you feel very close to the person you are writing to, use one of these closings: *Love, With love,* or *Your loving grandson.* You could also use one of these closings: *Sincerely, Your friend,* or *With thanks.*

As you fill out this first draft of your letter, be sure to get each part in the right place.

Grandparent Letter—First Draft

_____
(Today's date)

Dear_____:

(Indent here)

(News about yourself)

(Indent here)

(Reason for writing)

_____,
(Closing such as "Your friend")

_____
(Your name)

Grandparents' Communities

Show your rough draft to a grownup and ask these feedback questions.

- Did I use capital letters to begin names? the month? sentences?
- Did I use commas and periods where needed?
- Is my spelling correct?
- Is my meaning clear?

When the answer to all these questions is *yes,* copy your letter onto a clean sheet of writing paper. Put your letter and the community questionnaire from page 119 into your envelope. Don't forget to put a stamp on the envelope and then mail your letter.

Community Questionnaire

Thank you for participating in our classroom questionnaire. You will want to write your answers on a separate sheet of paper. Please put your name on that sheet so that it can be returned to your student correspondent after being shared with the class.

1. What town did you live in when you were eight or nine years old?
2. Was it a small town, medium-sized town, or large city at that time?

(Please answer any 8 of the following questions.)

3. What did most people in your community do to earn a living?
4. How did your family earn a living?
5. What was the main street in your community like?
6. What was the weather like where you lived? What do you remember doing to survive in that kind of climate?
7. How did people get from place to place within your community? How did you travel to another town?
8. What kind of home or apartment did you live in? How many rooms did it have? What was the room you slept in like? Did most of your friends live in similar homes?
9. Tell about any community celebrations you remember.
10. What was the grocery store where your family shopped for food like? How was it different from where you shop for food today?
11. How far away was the nearest hospital? Did you ever visit it? What was it like?
12. What school did you go to? Describe the classrooms and playground. What were your teachers like? How did you get to school?
13. What games did you like to play at home and at school?
14. What did people in your community do for recreation?
15. Was your community famous for a special food or dish? What was it?
16. Were there any inventions such as radio, television, the polio vaccine, or jet airplanes that changed life in your community when you were young? What were they? What changes did they bring about?

A Parent's Community

I. Preassessment Considerations

A. Note that the first part of this assignment is to be done in class with your students. During this period you may want to suggest that students with limited access to parents interview someone else's parent, an adult friend, or a teacher. Children who want to interview a parent not living at home should be encouraged to do their interviews by telephone.

B. You may want to warn students that their presentations will take some preparation time and should not be left to the last minute. If you plan to make the presentations a "big event," it might be wise to allow students extra time to prepare.

C. Students will enjoy this assignment. The children will find that the most challenging aspects of the assignment are summarizing parents' replies and making presentations.

II. Integration into the Classroom

A. **In-Class Preparation.** Before you send students home with their assignments, help them choose which questions they want to ask their parents, and help them think of additional questions they might want to add to the list. Decide together which, if any, of the presentation ideas is inappropriate due to lack of space, equipment, etc.

B. **Cluster Diagrams.** Ask students to fill out the following cluster diagram using the information they obtained from their interviews. Save the completed cluster for comparisons with the clusters of students' grandparents' communities and their own communities.

C. **Map Activities.** Using colored pins or stick-on dots, mark each parent's community on a national or world map. You may also want to do the same thing for grandparents' communities using a different color. What observations can your students make looking at the distribution of pins or dots?

D. **Preparing for Presentations.** You will want to set aside a safe place in the classroom for displaying mementos that are part of students' presentations. Be sure that children realize how precious these items are to their parents and that they treat them with the proper respect.

III. Extensions for GATE Students

A. **Charting Information.** Ask GATE students to represent interview data on a chart like the one suggested for use with grandparents' replies. To do this they must have access to interview sheets from all students.

Parent's Name	Community Name/Size	Home	Main Street	School	Grocery Store	Hospital

B. **Analyzing Charts.** When the students are finished with the chart, help them look for patterns, make comparisons, form generalizations, and make inferences based on the information they have collected. Compare this chart with the one done for grandparents.

C. **Organizing a Presentation Program.** GATE students can help you organize a "big event" based on this assignment.

1. Leaders: Have them find out who is doing what, plan the order of presentations, and make sure that everything is done on time.
2. Visual artists: Have them draw up an attractive program and create additional artwork for your display area (a Main Street mural, for example).
3. Performing artists: Have a child who is comfortable in the limelight act as master of ceremonies. You may want to divide this responsibility between two or more students.
4. Musicians: Have musically gifted students create a program of songs that were popular when their parents were in elementary school.
5. Mathematicians: Have GATE math students produce a profile of parents based on the interviews. They might represent their data on large bar graphs. Topics they might consider include the following.

   - Number of parents living east and west of the Mississippi.
   - Number of parents born in the US and in foreign countries.
   - Number of parents living in small, medium, or large towns.
   - Number of parents still living in childhood communities compared to those who moved to present locale as teens or adults.

Name

Date Due
Page 1 of 1

Parent's Community Cluster

Begin your cluster by filling in eight topics your parents talked about during your interview. Add as many details about these topics as you can remember. Topics include work, main street, climate, travel, home, celebrations, grocery store, hospital, school, games, entertainment, foods, and inventions.

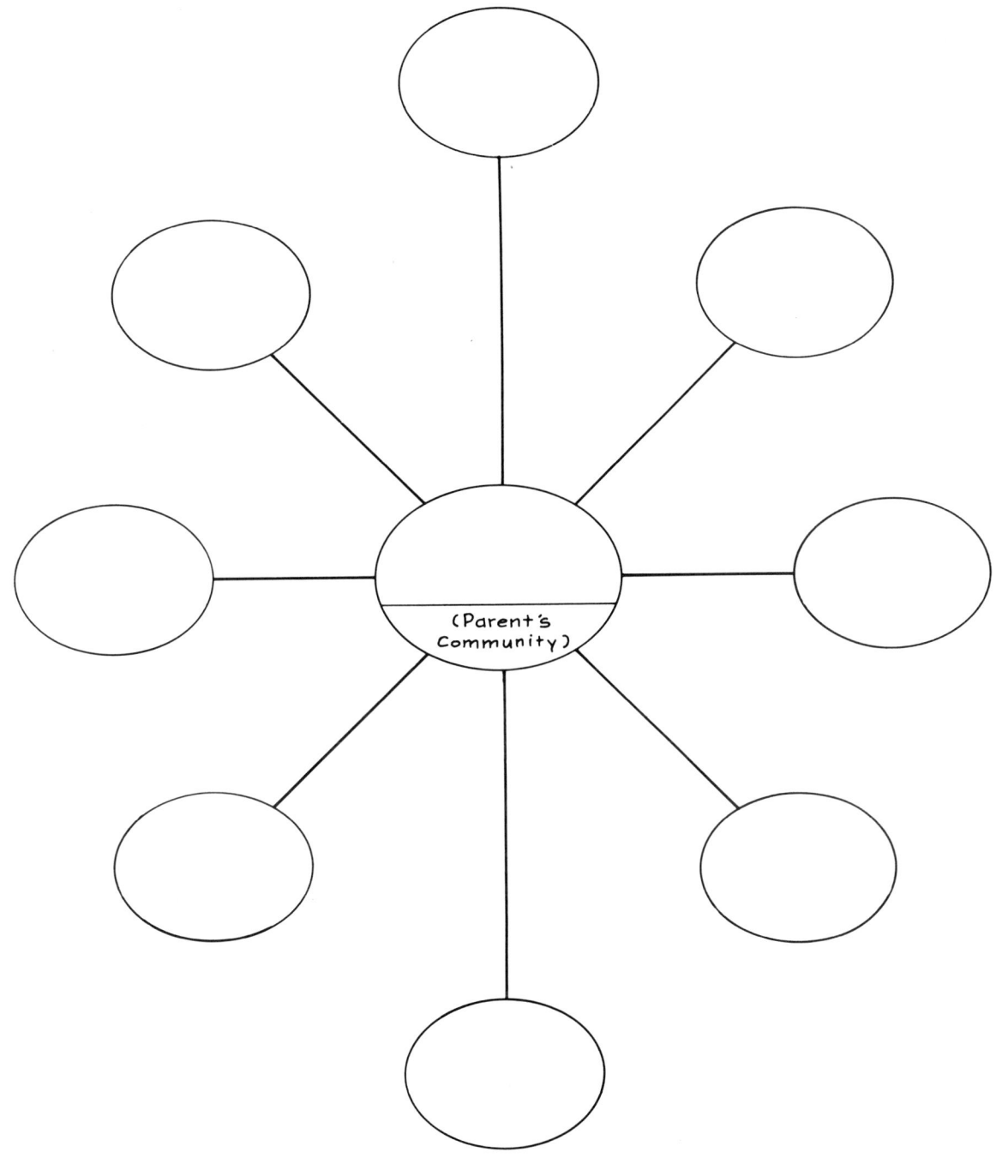

Unit Six — Parent's Community Cluster — 123

Name _____

Date Due _____

Parents' Communities

Where did your parents live when they were your age? In this assignment you will find out several things about a parent's childhood community.

Skills you will develop

- interviewing
- taking notes
- making a presentation

What you will need

- pencil
- parent to interview
- materials for a presentation

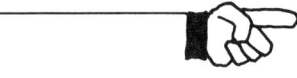

In Class with Your Teacher

1. With your teacher, read through the interview questions on pages 125–127. Circle the numbers beside the questions you would like to ask your parent. Choose at least six questions. If you or your teacher want to ask other questions, write them in the spaces for questions 15 and 16.

2. Look at the presentation ideas on page 128. Cross out any ideas that you and your teacher think are too hard to do in your class.

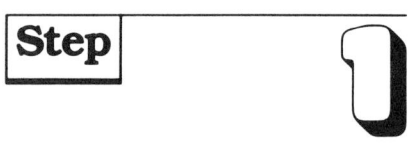

Preparing for Your Interview

An interview is a meeting for a special purpose. Make an appointment for an interview with a parent or other adult you live with. Try to find a time when you will not be interrupted. Use the telephone for your interview if your parent does not live at home with you.

Choose a quiet, comfortable place for your interview. Make sure you have something to write on such as a clipboard, table, or book. Have a pencil ready for taking notes. Your notes should be just a few words to remind you of your parent's answers. Write your notes in the space after each question.

Step	

Interviewing Your Parent

During your interview, ask the first two questions and the others you chose with your teacher. Then look at the presentation ideas on page 128 with your parent. Decide together what you will bring back to class.

Community Questionnaire

Name of person interviewed_____

What town did you live in when you were eight or nine years old?

Was it a small town, medium-sized town, or large city at that time?

(Ask the questions you circled in class.)

1. What did most of the people in your community do to earn a living?

2. How did your family earn a living?

3. What was the main street in your community like? Do you have any pictures of it?

4. What was the weather like where you lived? What clothes do you remember wearing in winter and summer?

5. How did you get from place to place in your community? How did you travel to other places?

6. What kind of home or apartment did you live in? Do you have any pictures of it? What was your room like?

7. Do you remember any community celebrations? What were they like?

8. What was the grocery store where your family shopped for food like?

9. What was the local hospital like? Were you ever a patient there? What do you remember most about being in the hospital?

10. What school did you go to? Can you describe the classrooms and playgrounds? What were your teachers like? How did you get to school?

11. What games did you play at home and at school?

12. What did your family do for entertainment and recreation?

13. Is your childhood community famous for a special food or dish? Do you know how to prepare it?

14. Can you remember anything that changed your community such as a new shopping center, highway, housing development, or business? What was it? What changes did it bring?

15. (Write your own question here.) _____
    _____

16. (Write your own question here.) _____
    _____

Before ending your interview, go over the presentation ideas on page 128.

Step  **Making a Presentation**

When you have decided on your presentation, gather the things you need. Bring them back to class to share.

Presentation Suggestions

Poster: Create a poster telling something about celebrations, food, entertainment, or other things you learned about in your interview.

Model: Bring in a model of a plane, train, or car similar to those your parent rode in as a child.

Tape recording: Record the person you interviewed telling an interesting story about a hospital stay, favorite teacher, or something else. Bring in a tape player or ask your teacher about using a school tape player.

Clothes: Share some clothes like those your parent wore at your age. You may even want to wear them to class. Tell your class anything you can find out about those clothes.

Home movies: Show some home movies of your parent at your age. Tell where the movie was made and what is going on. Check with your teacher about using a school projector first.

Recipe: Find a recipe telling how to make the special dish of your parent's community. Explain to your class how to make it. Better yet, make that dish and bring it to class to taste.

Old photos: Bring in old photos that show your parent's home and community. To keep the photographs safe, mount them on cardboard or put them in a photo album or photo cube.

Hometown news: Look through scrapbooks for any old newspaper clippings about things that went on in your parent's community. Plan to share them with the class. Because old clippings can be brittle, put them in an envelope to protect them.

Game: Learn one of the games your parent used to play. Show the class how to play it.

Shopping list: Make up a shopping list of your parent's favorite soft drinks, candy, and other treats when he or she was your age. Include the price of each item if your parent can remember it.

Skit: Create a skit in which you act the part of a teacher your parent remembers well. Run the class for a few minutes the way your parent's teacher might have done.

Collectors' items: Bring in any special things your parent has saved from his or her childhood. Look for toys, games, comic books, magazines, records, special collections, favorite books, posters, or other much-loved things.

My Own Community

I. Preassessment Considerations

A. In this assignment students are asked to gather various kinds of information about their communities. Although the process of collecting information is in itself worthwhile, it will be far more valuable if you provide class time for synthesizing the materials that students bring in. At least one hour should be set aside for this purpose on the day that bags arrive chock full of collected items.

B. Students will enjoy doing this assignment. The children will find that the most challenging parts of the assignment are ferreting out certain kinds of information about their communities and finding unique and interesting community news articles and souvenirs.

II. Integration into the Classroom

A. **Partner Categorizing Game.** Divide students into pairs. Have them cut out their labels and pictures, which they should pile on a desk along with their clippings and souvenirs. Ask students to sort their collected items first into two categories of their own choosing and then into three. Have them label their three piles with 3-by-5-inch cards and then tour the room to see how other students have sorted and labeled their items. You will see greater creativity in categorizing if you then give students time to resort their materials.

B. **Flash Speech.** Give students three minutes in which to choose the most interesting, unusual, or unique item in their bags and then prepare a short speech about that item. The speech should begin with a topic sentence stating what was selected followed by two or three supporting statements telling why this item was chosen. The reluctant speakers in your class will probably feel more comfortable if they are not the first to give their speeches.

C. **Bulletin Board Display.** The materials brought back by students can be used to make an interesting bulletin-board display about your community. You will need to provide the basic design framework. Your students will carefully select one item from each bag to become part of the display. A student gifted in art might be asked to print needed labels.

D. **Community Posters.** This activity is particularly valuable because it involves a great deal of analysis and synthesis, but it will also take more class time than the previous suggestions. The posters that come out of this activity, however, can be used to enhance relations between school and community by putting them on display in public places.

Begin by providing each student with a large piece of tagboard or butcher paper (at least 18 by 24 inches). Then have students choose two or three sheets of construction paper in different colors, preferably one light and one dark. If they have already colored the labels and pictures in their homework assignments, they should work with the same colors. Their posters will be more attractive if limited to two or three basic colors.

Next have students write the name of their community on the posters in large, attractive letters. Their efforts will be more interesting if you first show them examples of lettering found in advertising. Emphasize that the community's name should be the focal point of their posters by virtue of its size, style, color, and placement.

Continue by having students cut their construction paper into both large and small shapes, and then have them lay out the shapes on their posters in an interesting way. These colored areas will help students group items together. Now have them count the items in their bags, and challenge them to use only half (or less) for their posters. The chosen items should be arranged carefully on the colored-paper areas. Encourage students to experiment by turning some items sideways, overlapping items, and connecting items within an area in different ways. At this point they may also want to create labels for some grouping of items.

Before they glue anything down, have students work in pairs to improve each other's designs. These feedback questions will help them focus their comments.

- Did you leave empty space on your poster?
- Did you group items in a pleasing way?
- Are your items connected in some way?
- Did you limit yourself to two or three colors?
- Is your spelling correct?
- Is your writing neat?

Give students time to redesign their posters using this feedback. Then have them glue their items to the tagboard. Be parsimonious with the glue, but caution students to glue all the edges of each item so that corners and edges do not curl. The result should be posters that you will be proud to display throughout your community. (See "Extensions for GATE Students" for ideas on arranging such displays.)

E. **Group Presentations.** Divide your class into committees and give them 30 minutes to plan short presentations using the materials in their bags. Each committee should focus on a different topic such as work in our community, city government (including police and fire protection), historical sites, eating and shopping, and fun and amusement in our community. Or committees can explore more open-ended issues such as What makes our community beautiful? Why do people choose to live here? and Why do people want to work here?

F. **Cluster Diagrams.** Ask students to fill out the following cluster diagram using the information they collected about their own community.

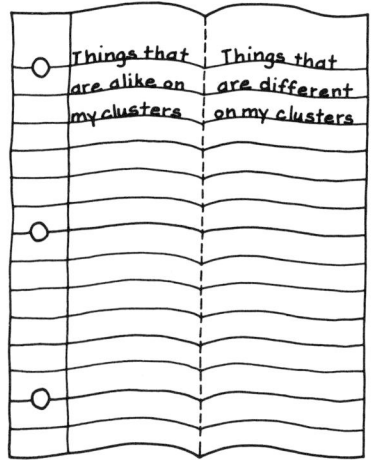

G. **Comparing Communities.** When students complete their own cluster, give them the diagrams they made about their grandparents' and parents' communities. Ask them to fold a sheet of paper in half lengthwise and on one side list things that are the same on two or three clusters. Things that are different should go on the other half. You may want to give each child a chance to share this analysis with the class. Is there a common thread running through the similarities and differences?

H. **Thank-you Notes.** Grandparents will appreciate getting thank-you notes that tell them how their letters were used by the class. To make this task easier, give students the study aids Writing a Letter and Addressing an Envelope from Unit 9.

III. Extensions for GATE Students

A. **Writing Comparison Paragraphs.** Academically gifted GATE students may use their comparisons of clusters as the basis of a comparison paragraph. Paragraph Planning in Unit 9 will facilitate the writing of a first draft. Here are some sample topic sentences to help students get started.

1. My community is a lot like my parent's community used to be.
2. My community is more like my grandparent's community than my parent's hometown.
3. The community I live in is different from my parent's in many ways.
4. This community has changed a lot since my grandparent grew up here.

B. **Poster Displays.** GATE leaders can organize the display of posters throughout the community. They might want to call local stores, libraries, public buildings, hospitals, banks, and other businesses to find places to show the posters. They should also make sure that posters get to the display places and are returned to their owners when the display period ends.

C. **New Students' Guide.** GATE students can organize the creation of a guidebook for new students in your school and community. The guide might include specific information about your school's rules, traditions, and special events. It could also have listings of resources throughout the community of special interest to children. These could include parks, playgrounds, good climbing trees, interesting stores, children's library, museums, sports organizations for children, youth organizations such as scouts and YMCA, and the best places to roller-skate.

D. **3-D Community Map.** Have GATE students lay out a large map of your community using tape on the classroom floor or chalk on the playground. They could begin by indicating major streets and natural landmarks. Everyone in the class can help fill out the map using boxes, cans, blocks, and other "found" materials to represent important community places such as the following.

- schools
- hospital
- parks
- fire station
- shopping areas
- pizza parlor
- radio station
- post office
- city hall or civic center
- playgrounds
- police department
- railroad station
- hamburger stop
- roller-skating rink

E. **Walking Tour.** Ask GATE students to plan and act as docents on a community walking tour. This tour might focus on local historical sites, public buildings, interesting businesses, a construction site, local parks, or other nearby areas of interest. Here are some of the things your planners/docents need to think about before the tour.

1. What points of interest should be included on the trip?
2. What will be the distance?
3. How long will the trip take?
4. What route will the class take coming and going?
5. Do we need to contact anyone at the places we will be visiting in advance?
6. Should we hand out maps or tour guides in advance?
7. What should we tell the class about each point of interest?

My Own Community Cluster

Name

Date Due

Begin your cluster by choosing eight of the topics listed here. Then add as many details about your community as you have room for. Topics include work, main street, climate, travel, home, celebrations, grocery store, hospital, school, games, entertainment, foods, and inventions.

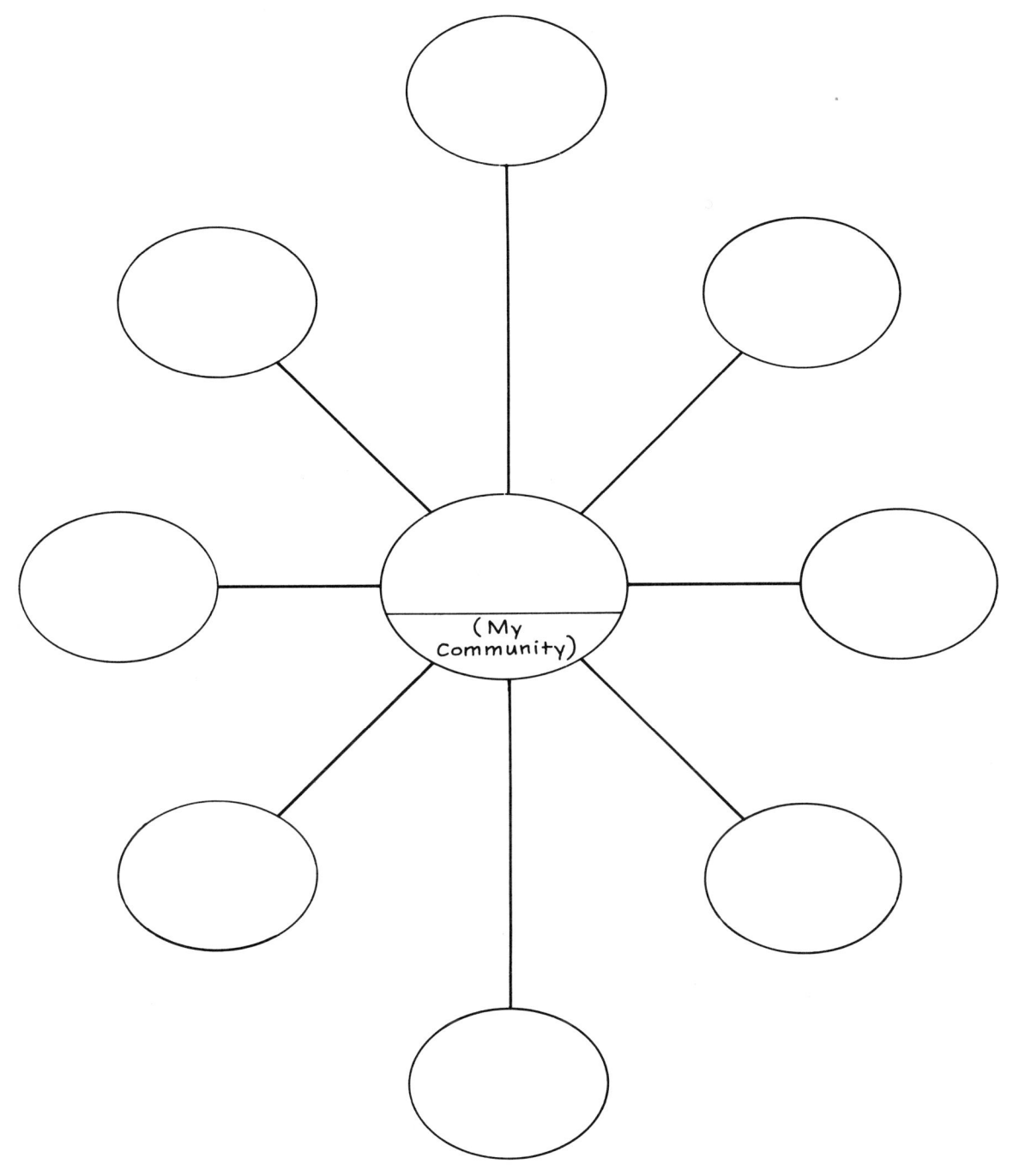

Unit Six

Name

Date Due

My Own Community

How well do you know your community? You will know it better by the time you have finished this assignment.

Skills you will develop

- collecting information

What you will need

- large shopping bag
- scissors
- crayons or marking pens
- local newspapers
- community souvenirs

Before you begin: Read steps 1 through 3. Find a large bag to use for collecting clippings and souvenirs. Start today!

Step 1

Gathering Information from Newspapers

This week you will gather information about your community. One place to look is in your local newspaper. For the next few days go through your papers and look for news about your community. Clip out any interesting items and put them in your bag. Here are some suggestions of things to cut out.

- A local weather report.
- Stories about what is happening in your community, such as new buildings and roads or bike lanes being built.
- Pictures of city officials such as the mayor or police chief.
- Stories about the local schools.
- News about people from your town who have become famous.
- Help-wanted ads of local businesses that are looking for workers.
- Local election results.
- Stories about local sports teams.
- Notices of things for people to do in their free time such as movies, classes, and plays.

Step 2: Collecting Community Souvenirs

As you go about your community for the next few days, look for souvenirs to collect. A souvenir is something you keep to remind you of an event or place. You might be able to find souvenirs like these to put in your bags.

- Leaflets telling about your community.
- Bus tickets or schedules.
- Photos or postcards of your community.
- Advertisements for community events.
- Fallen leaves or seedpods from local trees.
- A map of your community.
- Pressed flowers from local gardens.
- Official city stationery.

Step 3: Finding Out Community Facts

The labels and pictures in this step are missing some information. Fill in the missing facts using a pencil. If you don't know all the information asked for, you can look for help in the telephone book, at the library, at city hall, at the chamber of commerce, and from parents, neighbors, and friends.

When you have found your facts, have a parent or friend check your work. Are all the words spelled correctly? Have you used capital letters when you needed them?

Finally, go through the labels and pictures and color them in with crayons or marking pens. They will look better if you limit yourself to two or three colors.

Write the name of your community here.

Find out how many people live in your community. Write the number here.

How high is your community above the level of the sea? Write that number here.

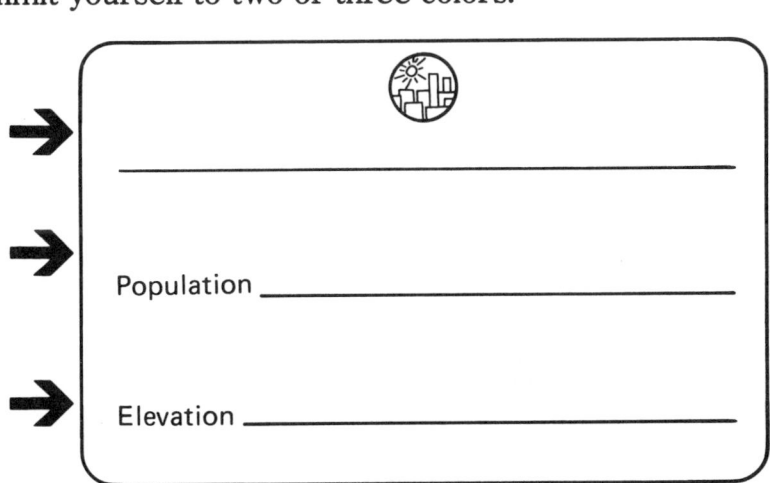

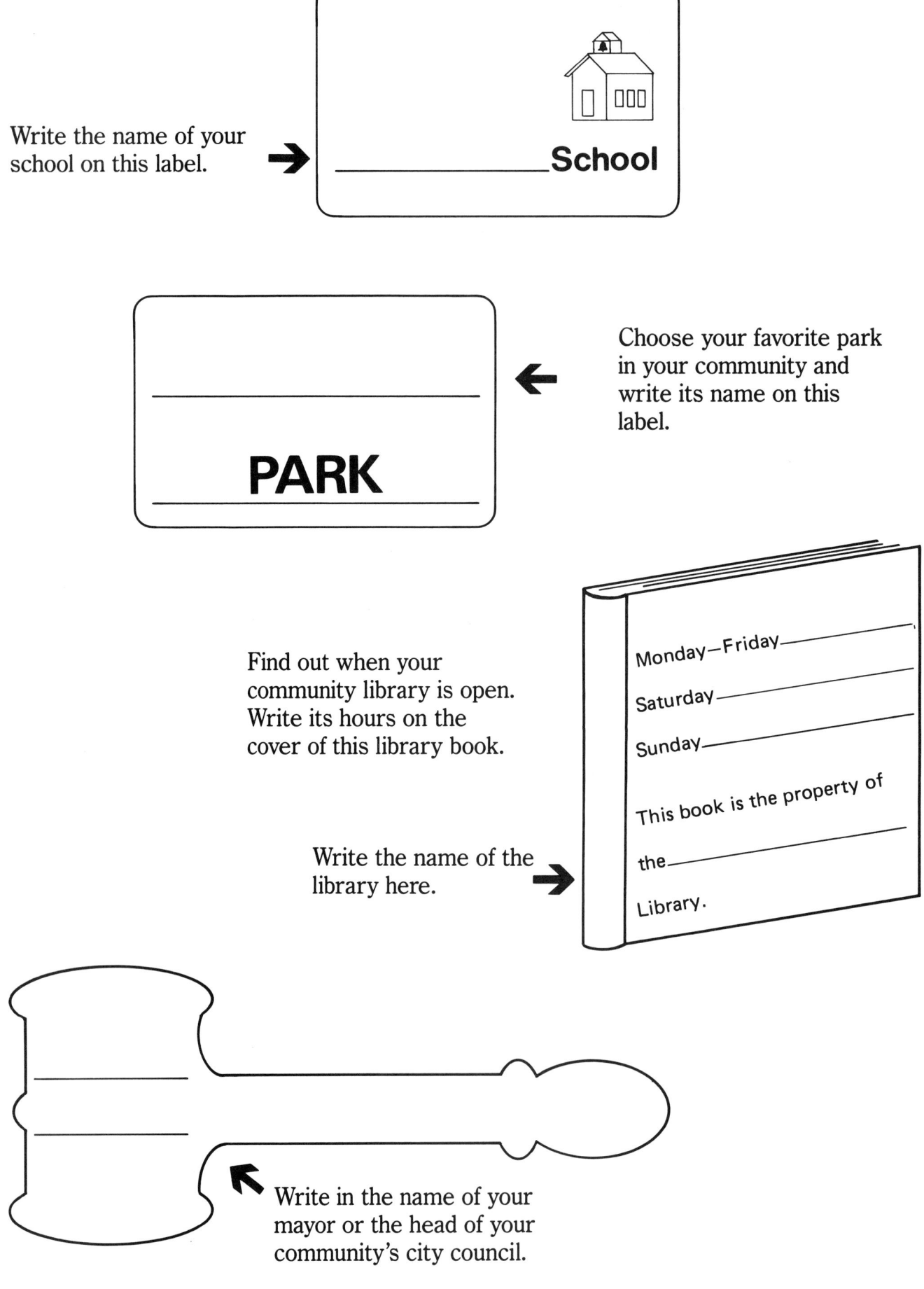

In Case of Fire Call
_____

Fill in the phone number you should call if you spot a fire.

Quiet Hospital Zone
_____
_____

Write in the name of the nearest hospital serving your area. →

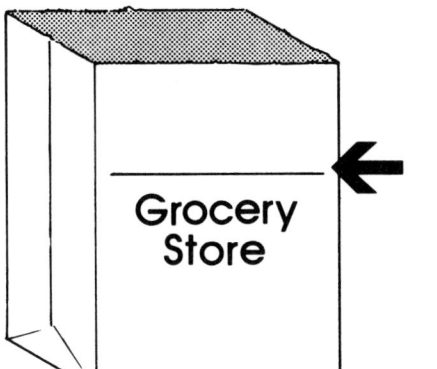

← Write in the name of the grocery store where your family shops. Put some groceries in the bag.

Fill in the name of an important place in the history of your community. Have you visited this place? _____

Historical Landmark
_____
_____
_____
_____
_____

Write in the phone number of the police or sheriff's department.

Call _____

Write the name of your favorite local restaurant above the plate. Then write on the menu the foods you like to eat there.

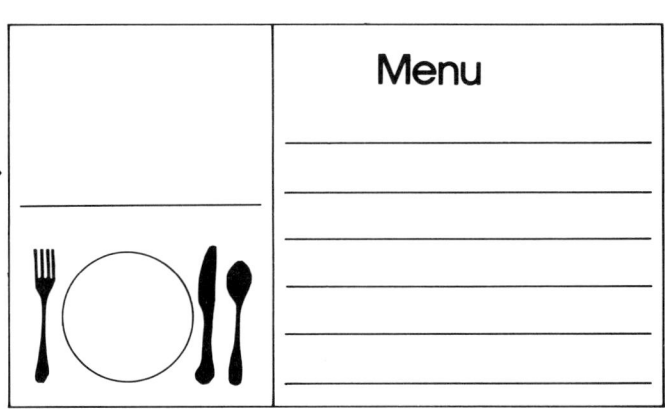

At the top of each store window write the names of three local stores where you shop. Then decorate the windows in a way that suits each store.

bag of info from newspapers; souvenirs, labels

Bring Back

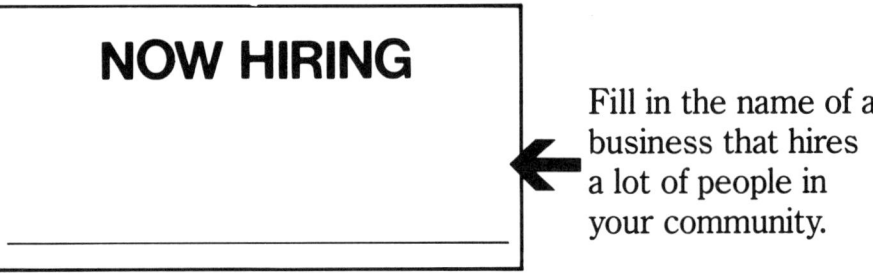

NOW HIRING

Fill in the name of a business that hires a lot of people in your community.

Bike Town—Planning a Community

I. Preassessment Considerations

A. This assignment is designed for children who will benefit from working as part of a team on an imaginative enrichment project. You may want to group students yourself to ensure a fertile mix of talents on each team.

B. This assignment can be done entirely in class if you prefer to use it that way. In this case children may want to bring materials from home to use on their projects. Or you may want to suggest that teams represent their plans with flour-and-salt maps.

II. Integration into the Classroom

A. **Motivation.** One way to spark enthusiasm for and creative thinking about this project is to spend time at the outset discussing such varied possibilities as an orbiting Bike Town, an undersea Bike Town, and a lunar Bike Town. During this discussion you will want to start students thinking about what elements make up a community. Should every community have a store, a fire station, schools, and a park, for example?

B. **Presentations.** Each team will enjoy sharing its planned community as well as finding out what other teams created. To prepare for their presentations, teams should pay close attention to the questions at the end of the assignment.

C. **Follow-up Discussions.** Choose one of the planned communities as the focus of a follow-up class discussion that extends the planning already completed. You might want to consider what kinds of laws and services would be important in this town, what problems students see with the present plans, and what kinds of environmental safeguards might be needed.

III. Extensions for GATE Students

A. **Team Leaders.** GATE leaders might be asked to head project teams in your classroom. Encourage your leaders to include every team member in discussions and in the creation of a report or display. Leaders should also make sure that their teams consider the questions at the end of the assignment before they make their presentations to the class.

B. **GATE Teams.** Because this is an open-ended assignment with a broad range of solutions to the basic problems, you may want to use it only with your GATE students. If so, you should expect your GATE students to analyze the problems in greater depth, to develop more involved plans, and to reach a more complex synthesis than your other students.

Name

Date Due
Page 1 of 2

Bike Town— Planning a Community

Can you imagine a community without cars? That is what you will be creating this week as you make plans for Bike Town.

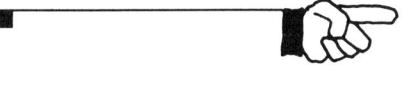

Skills you will develop

- working as part of a team
- analyzing
- problem solving
- planning
- synthesis

What you will need

- a friend to work with
- materials for displaying your plans

Congratulations! You have been chosen to prepare a plan for a new community. Your first task is to put together your team of community planners. Your teacher may have helped you form a planning team. If not, find a friend who would enjoy working with you on this project. Your friend does not have to be in your class to work as your planning partner.

Write your partner's name here: _____

Your assignment is to create plans for a new community called Bike Town. This community will have no private cars. Most people in Bike Town will get around by bike or on foot. You can display your plans in several ways. Here are some suggestions.

a. Draw a large picture of Bike Town. Show the location of buildings, roads, green areas, and so on.
b. Create a model of Bike Town on a large piece of cardboard. Use whatever materials you can find for trees, buildings, and other parts of your community.
c. Write a detailed description of Bike Town.
d. Make a map of Bike Town. It could be a road map that also shows where people live, shop, work, and play. Or you could make a relief map using a flour-and-salt dough to show how Bike Town might be laid out.

Unit Six

As you and your partner begin to plan this new community, think about these questions.

1. What kind of community will Bike Town be? A typical community with homes, workplaces, shopping areas, etc.? A "bedroom" community where people live who travel to other places to work? A recreational community where people come to have fun? A retirement community for senior citizens? A space community on the moon? Another kind of community?
2. Will this new community be large or small? Close together or spread out?
3. Where should Bike Town be located? On hilly or flat land? What kind of climate would suit Bike Town best?
4. How will people who can't use bikes get around in Bike Town?
5. What kinds of roads and traffic controls will Bike Town need?
6. Will any motorized vehicles such as buses, taxis, or trucks be needed in Bike Town?
7. What kinds of businesses might do well in Bike Town?
8. What kinds of emergency services (police, fire protection, hospitals, etc.) should Bike Town have?
9. What will people in Bike Town do for recreation and entertainment?

Your team will probably think of other questions to consider in your planning. The most important planning tool you have, however, is your imagination. So use it to create a new and wonderful place for people to live.

BUSINESS VENTURES

Scope

Seven assignments spanning seven to eight weeks. These assignments are sequential, but the sequence can be terminated at any point.

1. Goods and Services
2. Testing the Market I
3. Testing the Market II
4. Business Costs
5. Setting a Price
6. Open for Business
7. My Business Career

Additional Classroom Uses

Math ■ analyzing time ■ buying and selling stocks

Social Studies ■ committee work ■ analyzing tasks ■ dividing labor

Language ■ role playing ■ journal writing

Fine Arts ■ creating a program

Curriculum Integration

Math ■ adding and subtracting money ■ regrouping using money ■ financing a business with loans ■ using simple division ■ comparing ■ graphing ■ problem solving ■ chronological ordering

Social Studies ■ learning community economics ■ using economic/business concepts

Oral Language ■ telephone interviewing ■ personal interviewing ■ making sales presentations

Written Language ■ descriptive writing ■ analyzing feedback

Fine Arts ■ creating a product or service ■ synthesizing information using music, art, and writing

Challenges for GATE Students

■ analyzing ■ interviewing ■ making inferences ■ developing leadership skills ■ consulting

Dear Parent(s):

You now have a young businessperson in the family. Over the next few weeks your child will learn about the process of starting a new business. As part of this unit he or she will develop a variety of skills in the areas of math, language arts, fine arts, and social studies. Your child will also learn the importance of planning, analysis, careful scheduling of time, effective communication, and following through on commitments.

I suggest that you read each assignment as it comes home so that you will be ready to help when needed. In the first assignment, "Goods and Services," your child will need company while making a walking tour of a nearby shopping area. In "Testing the Market" you may be asked for your opinions of various business ideas. Your help will probably be most needed in the assignment "Business Costs," which requires students to analyze the cost of providing a specific product or service. Keep in mind as you help your child that the process of estimating costs is far more important than exact precision.

Some children may not like the suggestion that they limit their business to serving just three customers. For them the tangible reward of making money is a powerful and understandable motivation. Most students, however, don't have the time and energy during the school year to keep a business going. If your child is eager to continue, suggest opening the business again during a vacation period. Past experience suggests that children of this age will not be able to sustain their enthusiasm for a business beyond a week or two.

Sincerely,

Goods and Services

I. Preassessment Considerations

A. This assignment will work best with children whose parents are willing to go on a walking tour of a shopping area with them. If many of your students lack such support, you might consider doing the walking tour as part of a field trip or encouraging children to do their walking through the yellow pages of the local telephone book.

B. Most students will find that the most challenging parts of the assignment are categorizing sophisticated and often ambiguous data and displaying confidence during telephone interviews.

II. Integration into the Classroom

A. **Goods and Services Inquiry Game.** One way to introduce the concept of goods and services is to ask students to give you the names of local stores and businesses. Reply by telling them whether each business provides goods, services, or both. By the end of the game several students should be able to define goods and services. Better yet, some students may be able to provide ambiguous examples that provoke discussion about just what that business does provide.

B. **Walking Tour Field Trip.** A walking tour field trip is an excellent way to "kick off" the business ventures unit. Be sure students take their record sheets and pencils with them. You might want to break up into smaller groups if you have enough adults to do so. If students are unsure about what a business provides, encourage them to go inside and ask.

C. **Role-playing Telephone Interviews.** Students will have more confidence during their telephone interviews if they role-play an interview in advance. Whoever plays the role of the manager should throw the callers a few curves such as the following.

- "The manager is not in now. Can I have her call you later?"
- "I'm very busy now with a customer. Can you call back later?"
- "I'm the only person here now. Will I do?"

D. **Graphing Walking Tour Findings.** Each student might graph his or her tour findings in the following way.

Businesses providing goods: ☒☒☒☒☒☒☒☒☒☒
Businesses providing services: ☒☒☒☒
Businesses providing both goods and services: ☒☒

As you compare graphs, encourage students to look for patterns by asking questions like "Are there more service businesses in certain areas? Why?" Ask students to form hypotheses to explain patterns they see. For example, a student might reason, "I think there are so many goods businesses on Main Street because lots of people walk there and it is easy to park." Discuss how students might find evidence to support their hypotheses.

E. **Interview Follow-up.** In a follow-up discussion about the manager interviews you might want to ask some of these questions.

- "What things did managers like (dislike) about their businesses?"
- "What was most difficult for you about interviewing a stranger?"
- "Was the second interview easier than the first?"

III. Extensions for GATE Students

A. **Making Generalizations.** Ask two or three GATE students to read through the interview records in order to make a few generalizations about what managers of goods and services businesses like best and least about their businesses.

B. **Class Survey.** Ask one GATE student to survey the class to find out what kinds of businesses parents are working in at present or have worked in previously. The first challenge this student will face is defining his or her categories.

Name _____

Date Due
Page 1 of 4

Goods and Services

This week you will take a tour through a nearby shopping area and talk with managers of local businesses.

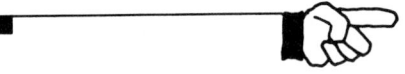

Skills you will develop

- collecting information
- using a telephone book
- categorizing
- interviewing
- evaluating

What you will need

- pencil
- paper
- telephone yellow pages
- telephone
- cooperative adult

Before you begin: Read steps 1 through 5. Make an appointment with your cooperative adult to take a walking tour of a nearby shopping area. You can go on to steps 3, 4, and 5 before you make your tour.

Step 1

Learning about Goods and Services

In order to earn money some businesses sell things, or goods. Goods sold in stores include food, clothing, books, records, and toys. Other businesses make money by doing things, or providing services. Such businesses might offer their customers haircuts, lessons, repair work, or banking services.

Some businesses offer both goods and services. Most restaurants sell food (a kind of good), but also provide a service by cooking the food and bringing it to the customer's table. Some jewelry stores sell watches (goods) and repair them when they are broken (a service). Gas stations often sell gas (a good) and repair cars (a service).

Think about some of the businesses you know. Fill in the name of one that sells goods. _____

Name one that sells services. _____

_____

Name one that provides both goods and services. _____

_____

Unit Seven

147

Step

Collecting Information About a Shopping Area

Do the businesses in your local shopping area provide goods, services, or both? To find out, make a date with your cooperative adult to take a walking tour of a neighborhood shopping area or shopping center. Before you go, make a record sheet like the one below.

As you tour the shopping area, write down the name of each business you pass by in one of your three categories. If you are not sure which category a business belongs in, your companion may be able to help you decide.

Walking Tour Record Sheet — Susan

Businesses Selling Goods	Businesses Selling Services	Businesses Selling Goods and Services
Classy Clothes	City Bank	Good Views Eyeglasses
Browser's Books	Dancing Wheels Roller Rink	Bountiful Bouquets Florists
Tommi's Tropical Fish Store	Silver Tongue School of Languages	Poortaste Pizza and Games
Bargain Boutique	Come Clean Drycleaners	Honest John's Gas and Car Repairs
Yum Yum Bakery	Dr. Sarah Plaque Dental Care	Get Well Pharmacy
	Happy Homes Real Estate	

Note: If you cannot take a walking tour, let your fingers do the walking in your telephone book. Use the yellow pages to find at least five examples of different businesses in each of your three categories.

Step  ## Interviewing the Manager of a Goods Business

Talk to the manager or person in charge of a business that sells goods. You may do this on your walking tour, or you can do a telephone interview.

Before you do your interview, practice asking the questions in the box to a friend or parent. When you do your real interview, record the manager's answers in the space provided.

Name of store_____

1. "Hello. My name is _____. I'm doing a business project for _____ School. May I please talk to the manager or the person in charge?" (If this person is not the manager, be sure to introduce yourself again when you do talk to the manager.)

2. "I know you're busy, but may I have just a few minutes of your time? I'd like to ask you some questions about your business." (If the manager is too busy, set up another time to talk, or call another business.)

3. "How would you describe your business?"_____
_____

4. "What brings customers to your store?"_____
_____

5. "What do you like best about your business?"_____
_____

6. "What do you like least about your business?"_____
_____

7. "Thank you for your time. You've been very helpful. Goodbye."

Step  ## Interviewing the Manager of a Service Business

For this next interview, talk to the manager or person in charge of a business that provides a service.

Name of Business_____

1. "Hello. My name is _____. I'm doing a business project for _____ School. May I please talk to the manager or the person in charge?"

2. "I know you're busy, but may I have just a few minutes of your time? I'd like to ask you some questions about your business."

3. "How would you describe your business?"_____
   _____

4. "What brings customers to your business?"_____
   _____

5. "What do you like best about your business?"_____
   _____

6. What do you like least about your business?"_____
   _____

7. "Thank you for your time. You've been very helpful. Goodbye."

Step 5 — Evaluating Your Interviews

When you have finished both interviews, answer these questions.

1. How did you feel before you began your first interview?
   _____
   _____

2. Was your second interview easier than your first?_____
   Why or why not?_____
   _____
   _____

3. What was the most interesting thing you learned from your interviews?
   _____
   _____
   _____

Bring Back: walking tour record sheet, homework assignment

Testing the Market I

I. Preassessment Considerations

A. This assignment can be done individually, in pairs, or in small groups. If students are working together, you may need to give them class time to design their products or services.

B. If safety is a concern in your area, be sure to talk about basic safety rules before children embark on neighborhood expeditions. Encourage students to take a buddy with them if they go door to door.

C. You will need a folder or envelope for collecting each student's business records beginning with this assignment. Those records will be used by students in "My Business Career."

D. The children will find that the most challenging aspects of this assignment are coming up with ideas for goods and services and communicating their business ideas to others.

II. Integration into the Classroom

A. **Business Brainstorming.** This assignment will be more fun if students have a chance in class to brainstorm with others about business ideas. Brainstorming works best in small groups. When the groups are finished, have each one share its best ideas with the class. Let students know that more than one child can pursue an attractive idea. If some students are torn between two ideas, suggest that they save one to test in the next assignment.

B. **Role Playing.** Market analysis interviews will go more smoothly if students rehearse in class. You might begin by having your more outgoing students interview you in front of the class. You will all have more fun if you invent some colorful characters for them to meet. During their interviews, students should be sure to communicate that they are not now selling a product or service but are simply looking for information. You might also want to emphasize the importance of common courtesies when dealing with adults.

C. **Marketing Resource Person.** The process of doing a market analysis will seem more important to students if you invite a marketing or sales person to class. Ask that person to describe how businesses use market analyses to test product and service ideas before going to market with them.

D. **Analyzing Market Information.** Students may do a better job of analyzing their market analysis charts if you do this part of the assignment in class. Using an overhead projector, go through one student's chart as a group, completing steps 3 and 4 together. If you plan to allow students to finish these steps in class, you may not want to send home the final page of the homework assignment.

E. **Revising Business Ideas.** Break your class into small groups to go over each other's business ideas and market analysis charts. Encourage students to give each other suggestions on how to improve their products or services.

III. Extensions for GATE Students

A. Hosting a Resource Person. A student with leadership skills might be asked to host a marketing resource person visiting your class. The host's duties will include (1) escorting the guest to the classroom, (2) briefing the guest about the class's business activities, (3) introducing the visitor to the class, and (4) thanking the resource person on behalf of the class when the visit ends. The host should also follow up with a thank-you note. See Writing a Letter and Addressing an Envelope in Unit 9.

B. Inference Activity. Present students with a list of goods and services and ask, "If you were conducting a market analysis for this product or service, what kinds of people would you want to interview, and where would you find them?" Here is a list of some ideas for products and services.

- peanut-butter-flavored chewing gum
- diaper cleaning service
- Flash-Bang video game
- rent-a-toy service
- deluxe car-cleaning service
- motorized roller skates

Name

Date Due

Testing the Market I

Over the next few weeks you will be going through the steps most businesspeople follow when starting a new business. You will begin by choosing a business and testing it.

Skills you will develop

- creating
- collecting information
- interviewing
- analyzing
- revising

What you will need

- pencil
- materials for a product or service

Before you begin: Read steps 1 though 4. Begin step 1 as soon as you can.

Creating a Product or Service

When a person wants to start a new business, he or she has to decide whether to sell a product or a service. That's the decision you need to make right now. If you think you would like to make a product for a new business, read the material in the next section. If you think you would like to offer a service, skip this section and read the section called "Service Business."

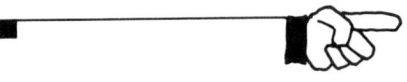

Product Business

Here are some ideas of products you could make for a business.

- snacks and foods
- stationery or cards
- books
- busy boxes for toddlers

- decorations
- birdhouses
- jewelry
- toys

When you have decided what your product should be, make just one sample item. If your product is a food, make just enough samples for three people to taste. Create something new for your product. Don't try to sell used items. And don't choose something so hard to make that your mom and dad have to do the work for you. Make your sample as attractive as you can so that people will be interested in it.

Service Business

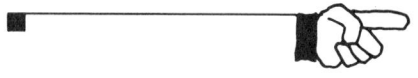

Here are some ideas for services you could provide in a business.

- reading aloud to someone
- cleaning
- shining shoes
- caring for pets
- doing yard work
- tending toddlers
- delivering something
- shoveling snow
- raking leaves

Make an attractive one-page leaflet about your service business. The leaflet should tell about your service. Try to include all the information people might want to know about your business *except* the cost of your service. You will set a price later. See the example below.

RANDY'S Animal Walking Service

A walk lasts 15 minutes. Monday to Friday 3:30 to 5:00 p.m.

I love animals!

STRONG LEASH PROVIDED

Step 3

Doing a Market Analysis

Before you go ahead with your business you need to know whether there is a market or need for your product or service. You will find this out by doing a market analysis.

Show your product or service leaflet to three people. Ask them the questions on the following market analysis chart. Record their answers in the space provided. Remember, you are *not* selling your product or service now; you are only collecting information.

If you do not feel comfortable going by yourself to interview people, take a friend or family member with you. You can also do your interviews by phone. In that case you will have to do a good job of telling about your product or service.

Market Analysis Chart

"Hello. My name is _____. I'm working on a business project for _____ School. I need your help with a market analysis for a new business. May I have a few moments of your time?" (Show the person your product or service leaflet. Then ask the questions below.)

	First Person	Second Person	Third Person
Would you buy this product/service?			
What would you expect to pay?			
How many would you buy? *or* How often would you want this service?			
How could this product/service be improved?			
"Thank you for your time and interest."			

Testing the Market I

Step 3 — Analyzing Your Chart

Look over your market analysis chart and answer these questions.

- How many of the people you interviewed said they might buy your product or service?_____

- Were the prices they said they would pay about the same or different?_____

Step 4 — Revising Your Product or Service

Show your product sample or service leaflet to a friend or family member. Choose someone whom you did not interview for your market analysis. Ask that person how you could make your product or service more attractive. Look over any ideas for improvements you got in your market analysis. Then answer this question.

If you were to make this product sample or service leaflet again, what would you do to improve it?_____
_____
_____

Testing the Market II

I. Preassessment Considerations

There are several reasons for having students complete a second market analysis. First, a second analysis gives students whose initial ideas did not look promising a chance to try something else. Second, students who tested a product now have an opportunity to try out a service and vice versa. Third, students will find both their interviewing and analytical skills improving as they go through the process again. Finally, each student's potential for success in starting a business is improved if he or she has a choice between two tested business ideas.

II. Integration into the Classroom

A. Business Inquiry Game. In this "What's My Line"-type game, students try to guess what kind of business the contestant is considering. Have the first contestant stand while students take turns asking *yes*- or *no*-type questions.

Examples: "Do you plan to offer a service in your business?"
"Can you eat your product?"
"Would kids want your service?"

Each *yes* answer buys the questioner another question. A *no* answer moves the questioning along to someone else. Sooner or later students will have enough information to make guesses about the specific business being considered. After playing the game once as a class, you might want to break the class into smaller groups to give more children a turn at being contestants and questioners.

B. Product Guessing Game. This game works best if several students have brought in sample products. Put those products in the center of a circle of students. Ask one student to pick a product in his head, keeping the choice a secret. That student then gives the class a clue about the product he has picked.

Examples: "This product is larger than a raisin."
"This product smells good."

More and more clues are offered until someone correctly guesses the product. The challenge in this game is to offer accurate but subtle clues that don't give away the answer at once. The game can be repeated until most of the items in the circle have been chosen.

C. Service Charades. Students who are thinking of offering a service might be asked to pantomime their services while the class tries to guess what each one is.

D. Revising Business Ideas. Once again your students will benefit from meeting together to discuss and revise their business plans.

E. Forming Business Groups. Before you move on to the next assignment, consider grouping some students to work together in setting up their businesses. Students with similar businesses may want to team up. Children unhappy with the results of their market testing may want to link up with more promising ventures. Some children, however, may prefer to pursue their ideas solo.

III. Extensions for GATE Students

A. Interviews With Business Owners. Your GATE students should be able to plan and carry out an extended interview of a business owner. The first step might be for the students to meet together and make up a list of questions to ask. Topics they might want to consider exploring include the following.

- Why did you choose this business?
- Where do you get most of your business ideas?
- Why did you select this location?
- Did you do a market analysis before you started your business?
- How have you improved your business since you started it?
- What changes would you like to make in the future?
- What qualities do you look for in your employees?
- What do you like about owning your own business?
- What don't you like about it?

Next, students will need to identify business owners to interview. You may want to steer some of your students toward local businesswomen as a way of providing positive role models of women in the business world. During their interviews, students may want to make brief notes that can serve as the basis of a report on their interviews.

B. Business Survey. Have GATE students take a survey among their friends and neighbors to find out what grocery store or service station people like best and why. The information collected could be displayed in a graph and made the basis of an interesting discussion on the elements that contribute to a successful business.

Name

Date Due

Testing the Market II

Try out another business idea by creating a new product or service and testing the market again.

Skills you will develop

- creating
- collecting information
- interviewing
- analyzing
- revising
- making choices

What you will need

- Testing the Market I assignment
- pencil
- materials for a product or service

Before you begin: Read steps 1 through 5. Begin step 1 as soon as you can.

Step 1

Creating a Product or Service

Think of a new product or service idea for a business you could run. It should be different from the idea you tested in your last market analysis. Look back to step 1 of "Testing the Market I" for ideas. Create a sample product or leaflet describing your service to use for a new market analysis.

Unit Seven

Step 2: Doing a Market Analysis

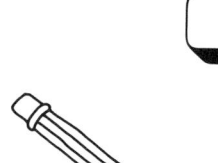

Talk to three people about your new business idea. Ask these questions and record their answers in the space provided.

Market Analysis Chart

"Hello. My name is _____. I'm working on a business project for _____ School. I need your help with a market analysis for a new business. May I have a few moments of your time?" (Show the person your product or service leaflet. Then ask the questions below.)

	First Person	Second Person	Third Person
Would you buy this product/service?			
What would you expect to pay?			
How many would you buy? *or* How often would you want this service?			
How could this product/service be improved?			

"Thank you for your time and interest."

Step 3: Analyzing Your Chart

Look over your market analysis chart and answer these questions.

- How many of the people you interviewed said they might buy your product or service? _____

- Were the prices they said they would pay about the same or different? _____

Step 4: Revising Your Product or Service

Show your product sample or service leaflet to a friend or family member. Choose someone whom you did not interview for your market analysis. Ask that person how you could make your product or service more attractive. Look over any ideas for improvement you got in your market analysis. Then answer this question.

If you were to make this product sample or service leaflet again, what would you do to improve it? _____

_____

Step 5: Selecting the Best Business for You

Which of the two business ideas you have tested would you like to use to start a new business? Before you decide, think about the following questions.

- Which product or service would you most enjoy providing?
- Which product or service did the people you interviewed seem more likely to want?
- Which product or service needs to be improved most to be successful?
- Which product or service can you provide in a reasonably short amount of time?

Write your final choice for a new business here. _____

_____

assignment, sample product, or service leaflet

Bring Back

Business Costs and Setting a Price

I. Preassessment Considerations

A. These two assignments will not be difficult for students providing simple services or making products using just a few materials. For children baking cookies or making more complicated products, parental assistance will be almost essential in estimating costs. In such cases you may want to send home a note to parents something like this one.

> Dear Parent(s):
> In the next two business assignments your child will be asked to estimate the cost of materials and labor needed to serve three customers in his or her business. Your help will be very important to your child.
> As you work through these assignments together, keep in mind that exact precision is not necessary. What is important is that your child gains experience in the process of making estimates. At the same time he or she may come to appreciate that businesspeople have to consider costs carefully when starting new ventures.

B. If you decide that these assignments are too difficult for some students, skip them and go on to "Open for Business." You will need to help these students set prices using the information they gathered in their market analysis and your own good common sense.

II. Integration into the Classroom

A. **Checking the Math.** On both these assignments you may want to have students work in pairs to check each other's math. This is a logical occasion for using calculators if they are available in your classroom.

B. **Discussion of Business Costs.** You may want to talk with your class about other costs businesspeople have to consider besides materials and labor. Such costs might include the following.

- rent
- phone
- water
- insurance
- supplies
- equipment
- travel expenses
- heat
- electricity
- taxes
- business licenses
- postage
- advertising
- cleaning fees

C. **Assembly Line Experiments.** American industry pioneered the use of assembly lines to produce goods more efficiently. In this two-day activity, students will begin to see the virtues as well as the problems of dividing work up in this way.

1. On day 1 give each student the paper model on page 165 to cut out, color, and assemble with glue. Be very general in your instructions on the order in which to do these steps. Have each student time how long it takes to complete one model. (An alternative is to have students find out how many models they can complete in a fixed time.)

2. On day 2 begin with a short discussion of how assembly lines work. Then divide the class into groups of five or six students to set up their own assembly lines for making paper models. Each group should decide for itself how to divide up the work. Keep track of the time worked and the number of models completed by each assembly line so that you can compare their output with the time it took individuals to finish a model.

3. As you discuss this activity, you may want to ask some of these questions:

- What are the advantages of an assembly line?
- How do the assembly-line models compare with the models you produced by yourselves?
- Did you have any special problems working together on an assembly line?
- Did you like working on an assembly line?
- What ways of organizing helped some groups produce more cars than others?
- What slowed some groups down?

III. Extensions for GATE Students

A. **Efficiency Experts.** While most of the children are working in assembly lines, one or two GATE students could be asked to visit each team, observe how they divided up the work, and note any problems. The observers could then suggest modifications in assembly-line procedures, or they could wait and report their observations to the class during the assembly-line discussion.

B. **Cost Consultants.** GATE students might be asked to serve as consultants to those students who had difficulty with these assignments or who are concerned with the costs of their products or services.

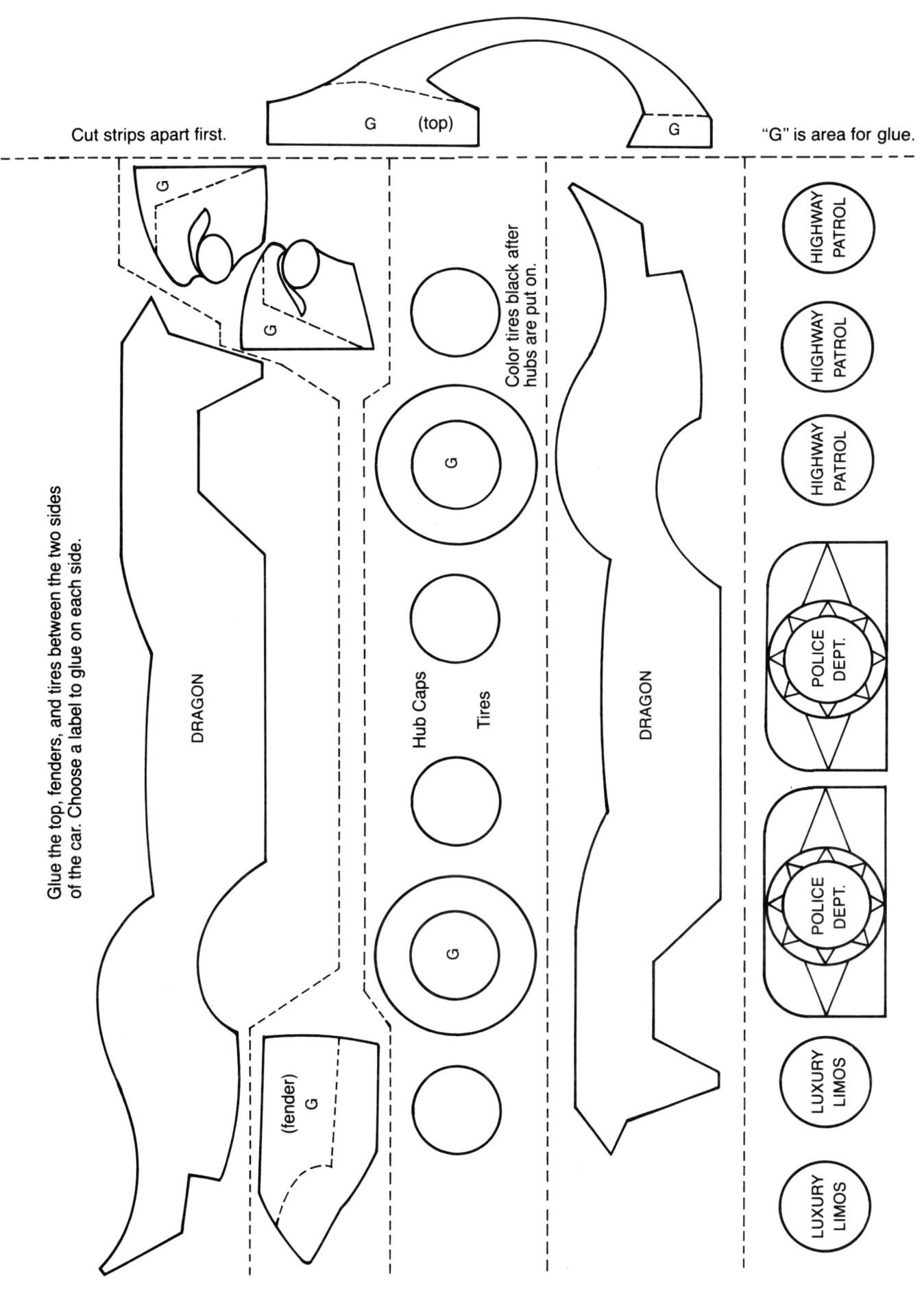

Name

Date Due
Page 1 of 3

Business Costs

In this assignment you will find out how much it will cost you to start a small business.

Skills you will develop

- estimating
- adding
- analyzing
- collecting information

What you will need

- pencil
- helpful adult

Before you begin: Read steps 1 and 2. Make an appointment with a grownup who can help you with step 2.

Step 1

Estimating Labor Costs

In the last assignment you chose the product or service you would like to provide in a new business. Do you have any idea how much it would cost you to start this business? You need to think about two kinds of costs: materials costs and labor cost.

Labor cost is the money paid to workers in a business for the time they work. You should plan to pay any worker you hire 1¢ per minute, or 60¢ per hour. If you do all the work yourself, pay yourself 60¢ an hour for your labor.

If you had three customers, how long would it take you to make your product or provide your service?

Write your estimate here. _____
Use this estimate to figure out your labor costs. Here's how.

Example: Maria estimated that it would take her 2 hours and 30 minutes to make three bird feeders. She added up her labor costs in this way.

```
 .60   (first hour)
 .60   (second hour)
 .30   (30 minutes)
-----
$1.50  (total labor cost)
```

Add up your labor costs on the back of this paper.

Write the total here. _____

Step  **Estimating Materials Costs**

The chart on page 168 will help you add up your materials costs. In a service business, materials costs are often small. If you are making a product, you may have a long list of materials you need.

In the first column marked *materials* on the chart, list all the things you will need to make your product or provide your service. Include things that you may already have around the house like marking pens, paper, flour, or cleaning liquid. You do not need to list tools and equipment that you can borrow and return like a lawnmower, sewing machine, or dog leash.

In the column marked *amount*, write how much or how many of each item you will need for three customers. Make your best estimate.

Now ask a grownup to help you. In the last column marked *cost*, write how much each item will cost. You will have to estimate if you need only a small amount of something like a teaspoon of salt. You may have to call or visit a store to get prices for some items. Found items like seedpods or pebbles will cost you nothing. The same is true of recycled items like paper-towel rolls. When you have finished, add up all your materials costs.

Materials	Amount	Cost
Toilet paper rolls	3	$ .0
Box of birdseed	1	$ .69
Sticks	3	$ .0
Yarn	1 ball	$ .59
Honey	1 jar	$1.25
Total materials costs		$2.53

Describe your business: _____

Materials	Amount	Cost
		$.
		.
		.
		.
		.
		.
		.
		.
		.
		.
		.
		.
		.
		.
		.
		.
		.
		.
Total materials costs		$.

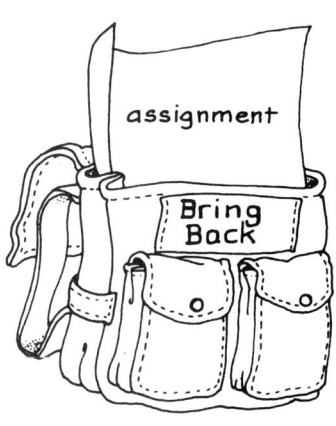

Name

Date Due
Page 1 of 3

Setting a Price

Sometimes the most difficult part of starting a new business is deciding how much to charge customers. This assignment will help you set a price for your product or service.

Skills you will develop

- making decisions
- adding
- dividing
- comparing
- revising

What you will need

- Business Costs assignment
- pencil
- market analysis chart for your product or service

Before you begin: Read steps 1 through 4.

Making Decisions—How Much Profit?

Setting a price for a product or service is not always easy. If the price is set too high, people may not buy the product or service. If it is set too low, it may not cover the costs of providing that product or service.

Your price should cover the costs of your materials and labor. It should also include some profit for you. Profit is the money left over after the business costs have been paid. Profit is a businessperson's reward for starting a business.

Decide now how much profit you would like to make after selling your product or service to three customers. Write the amount here. $_____.

Setting a Price

To set a price for your product or service, add together your materials costs, estimated labor cost, and the profit you would like. You will need your Business Costs assignment for the first two numbers.

Unit Seven

Materials costs for three customers $_____._____

Estimated labor cost for three customers $_____._____

Profit from step 1 +$_____._____

Total $_____._____

Divide the total by 3 to get the price for your product or service. Use a calculator or ask a grownup for help if you have trouble dividing.

$_____._____ ÷ 3 = $_____._____
(costs and profit)   (price)

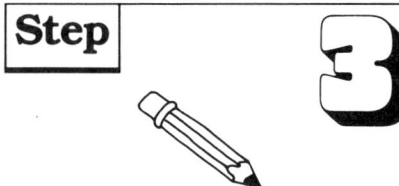

Step 3 — Revising Your Price

Is this a good price? Compare your price from step 2 to the prices people said they would pay in your market analysis.

- If your price seems about right, go on to step 4.
- If your price seems too low, you may not be giving yourself enough profit. Write a revised profit amount here. $_____._____
- If your price seems too high, think about these questions.

   1. Are you asking for too much profit? If you are, write a revised profit amount here. $_____._____
   2. Can you cut your costs by using less expensive materials or more free things? If you can, use your Business Costs assignment to help you revise your materials costs. Write your revised total here. $_____._____
   3. Can you cut your labor costs by doing things more simply? If you can, write your revised labor cost estimate here. $_____._____

"If I use cord instead of braiding yarn, I can cut my labor costs."

| Step |  | **Making a Business Plan** |

Bring all your figures together in this business plan. If you revised your costs or profit in step 3, use the revised amounts in the plan.

Business Plan

Product or service _____

Costs for serving three customers:

    Materials $_____._____

    Labor $_____._____

Profit   +$_____._____

Total costs and profit $_____._____ ÷ 3 =

Final price $_____._____

Open for Business

I. Preassessment Considerations

A. If safety is a concern in your community, encourage students to take a companion with them when they go out to sell their products or services. Rather than going door to door, they might limit their sales calls to people they know and/or to protected areas such as their own apartment buildings, the school, and parents' places of employment. Sales can also be made by telephone.

B. The children will find that the most difficult parts of this assignment are creating an effective sales presentation and then following through on orders and loan repayments.

II. Integration into the Classroom

A. **Sales Presentations.** Some students will do a better job of writing a sales presentation if they have time to share their first drafts with other students in feedback groups. The first three questions in step 2 will guide the groups in their discussions.

B. **Salesmanship.** Invite an effective salesperson to your class to talk about his or her work and what makes a good salesperson. You may want to leave time for some students to share their sales presentations and have this resource person make suggestions for improvement.

C. **Financing Businesses.** Most individual businesses can be financed through small, personal loans. If your class is composed of several group businesses, students might consider selling stock at 10¢ per share to raise funds. Students will have to decide what sort of dividend to promise if the venture succeeds (perhaps 1¢ per share) and should plan to redeem all stock when the venture ends. To make this financing plan work, the business group must decide how many shares to offer at what price, make the stock certificates, find buyers among friends and family, and keep records of who has purchased stock so that it can be repurchased at the end of the business. If the business succeeds, stockholders should be repaid in full, plus they should earn a dividend on their investment. If the business does not do well, the stock will become worthless.

D. **Problem Sharing.** Throughout this week give students time to talk about their experiences and any problems they encounter. This discussion may help procrastinators get on with the job as well as give you a chance to monitor students' business activities.

E. **Customer Portraits.** For a writing project, have students fill out a cluster diagram on one of their customers. Subtopics might include how the customer looked and acted, what he or she ordered, where the customer lived or worked, what that person said about the product or service, and any curious things that happened during the transaction. Students can use this information to write a well-organized paragraph entitled "My Favorite Customer." You may want to use the Cluster Diagram and Paragraph Planning from Unit 9 to assist students.

III. Extensions for GATE Students

A. **Getting Organized Skit.** If you have students gifted in the performing arts, ask them to plan and present a short skit on the well-organized versus the poorly organized salesperson when meeting a potential customer. This presentation can lead into a discussion of ways for students to organize themselves with a calendar, order blanks, etc., when going out to sell.

Name

Date Due

Page 1 of 4

Open for Business

The time has come to open your business. First you will take orders from customers, and then you will fill those orders.

Skills you will develop

- communicating—selling
- getting feedback
- organizing yourself
- following through

What you will need

- pencil
- paper
- materials for your product or service

Before you begin: Read steps 1 through 5. You will need to schedule your time carefully.

Step 1

Creating a Sales Presentation

Are you ready to start your business? Your first job is to look for three customers who would like to buy your product or service. Why just three? The reason is that during the school year you have many other activities going on and probably won't have time to run a business as well. If you decide you like being a businessperson, plan to open your business again this summer when you have more free time.

Before talking to possible customers, think about what you could say to persuade them to buy your product or service. Here are two examples of sales presentations.

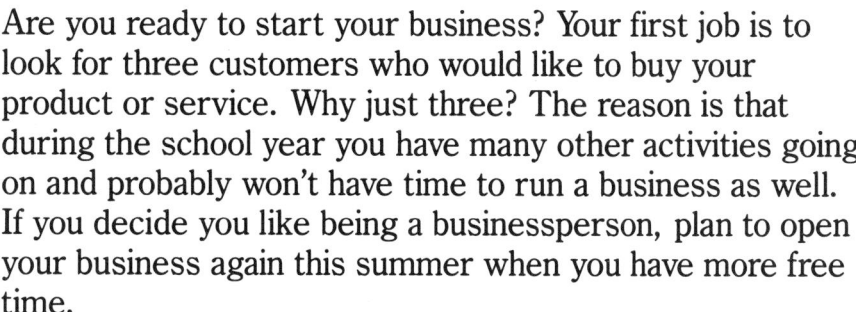

Hello. My name is John Garcia. As part of project for Franklin School I am starting a dog-walking business. Did you know that dogs need regular exercise? Without it they get fat, lazy, and bored. That's when they dig up the yard. I am experienced at walking dogs. I have a German shepherd at home. I will walk your dog for at least 15 minutes for only 50¢. I have my own leash or will use yours. Would you be interested in my service?

Unit Seven

Hello. My name is Jennifer Barnes. I'm starting a business as part of a project for Edison School. I wondered if you would like to buy some of my fresh-from-the-oven granola cookies. I make them myself using all natural ingredients. They cost $1.50 for a plate of 24 cookies. Would you like to try one to see how delicious they are? I'm taking orders today.

Write the first draft of your sales presentation here.

_____
_____
_____
_____
_____
_____
_____
_____
_____
_____
_____
_____

Step 2

Getting Feedback on Your Presentation

Try out your sales presentation on an adult. Then ask these questions.

- Is my presentation easy to understand?
- Have I left out any important information?
- Can you suggest any colorful words I could include to persuade customers to buy?

Use any suggestions you like to revise your sales presentation. Then discuss these questions with your adult.

- What should I wear when I visit possible customers?
- Where should I look for customers?
- Should I take someone with me when I go out selling?
- What is the best time to go out selling?
- Are there any other things I should remember when I go out to sell?

Step  **Organizing Yourself to Meet Customers**

You will want to appear very organized and businesslike when you go out to take orders. This will be easier if you make three order forms to take with you. Here are two examples. Your order forms may call for other information you will need to fill your orders.

Product Order Form

Customer's name_____

Address_____

Phone_____

Delivery date_____

Amount ordered_____

Description (color, size, flavor, etc.)

_____

Price_____

Service Order Form

Customer's name_____

Address_____

Phone_____

Appointment for service

Date_____

Time_____

Price_____

You should also take a calendar with you or make a schedule for the week to take along. Make a note of any after-school activities you have this week. Your calendar will help you and your customers decide when you should deliver your product or provide your service.

Here is a checklist of things you should take with you when you go selling.

☐ Sample product or service leaflet
☐ Sales presentation
☐ Three order forms
☐ Calendar or schedule

Step 4 — Following Through on Your Orders

As you begin filling your orders, you may need to borrow money to buy materials. Or you may want to borrow materials or equipment from your family. When you talk to someone about borrowing, show that person your business plan and your orders. Tell what you need to borrow and when you will pay back the loan. If that person agrees to loan you what you need, fill out a promissory note. A promissory note is simply a promise to pay back a loan. Your note might look like one of these examples.

```
PROMISSORY NOTE

I promise to pay Mom
$1.59 for her box of raisins
by February 15.
            Jennifer Barnes
```

```
PROMISSORY NOTE

I promise to return
Mr. Gomez's dog leash
by May 7.
            John Garcia
```

You may decide to hire a friend or someone in your family to help you fill your orders. If you do, offer to pay your worker 1¢ per minute, or 60¢ per hour.

It is important to fill your orders on time. If you fall behind, be sure to phone your customers and set up a new time to deliver your product or provide your service.

Your customers should pay you when you have filled their orders. Use that money to pay back any loans and pay any workers you hired. The money that is left is your pay for your time and your profit. You have earned every penny of it.

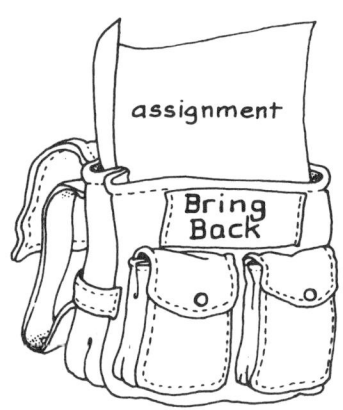

My Business Career

I. Preassessment Considerations

A. Before you send this assignment home decide when and where students will make their presentations. If you want to invite parents or another class to be part of this occasion, appropriate arrangements will have to be made in advance.

B. To complete the first step in this assignment, students will need their folders containing their business records.

C. The children will find that the most challenging part of this assignment is selecting what parts of their experience to focus on in their presentations.

II. Integration into the Classroom

A. **Clustering Business Experiences.** You may want to begin this assignment in class by giving students their business records and having them complete their business clusters. If time permits, have each child share his or her cluster with someone else.

B. **Selecting Presentation Ideas.** Either when sending this assignment home or shortly thereafter, you might want to find out what kind of presentations your students are planning to make. If you find yourself faced with 30 mobiles, you may want to encourage some students to consider something else. This would also be a good time to make your quality standards known.

C. **Business Convention.** Students will be more motivated to make high-quality presentations if their work is made part of a business convention attended by parents or other classes. At this convention you will need to have an area for visual displays. During the convention each student should talk to the audience about his or her work. This might take the form of reading a poem, presenting a play, describing a game, or showing off a book.

D. **Feedback Groups.** Before your business convention give students a chance to practice their presentations in front of a group of students. The feedback questions in step 6 may help guide the groups' discussions.

III. Extensions for GATE Students

A. **Organizing a Business Convention.** Your GATE students can help with the organization of a business convention by doing some or all of the following.

   1. Survey students to find out what kind of presentation each student is planning to bring to class.
   2. Prepare a display area for presentations.
   3. Work with students bringing visual and written presentations to help them decide what they want to say about their work.
   4. Make up an order of presentations, and write a program for the convention.
   5. Create illustrations for the program.
   6. Supervise the writing of invitations to the convention.
   7. Write a letter to a local newspaper inviting a reporter to cover the convention.
   8. Write thank-you letters as appropriate.

Name

Date Due

Page 1 of 6

My Business Career

What did you learn about running a business? Did you have any surprising experiences? All this and more should go into your report on your business career.

Skills you will develop

- ordering
- clustering
- making decisions
- planning
- synthesizing
- getting feedback
- making a presentation

What you will need

- your business records
- pencil
- materials for your presentation

Before you begin: Read steps 1 through 6.

 **Ordering Your Business Records**

In this assignment you will prepare a report on your business career to share with your class. To get started, collect your business records. These include your business plan, market analysis charts, sales presentation, materials costs chart, order forms, and any promissory notes you wrote.

Lay out your records on a table in the order of what you did first, second, third, and so on. This ordering will help you remember all the things you have done during your business career.

 **Clustering Your Business Experiences**

Use the cluster diagram on page 184 to help you organize your business experiences in a different way. You may want to add other topics to the cluster. Try to include lots of interesting details. Use the example on the next page to help you.

Unit Seven

181

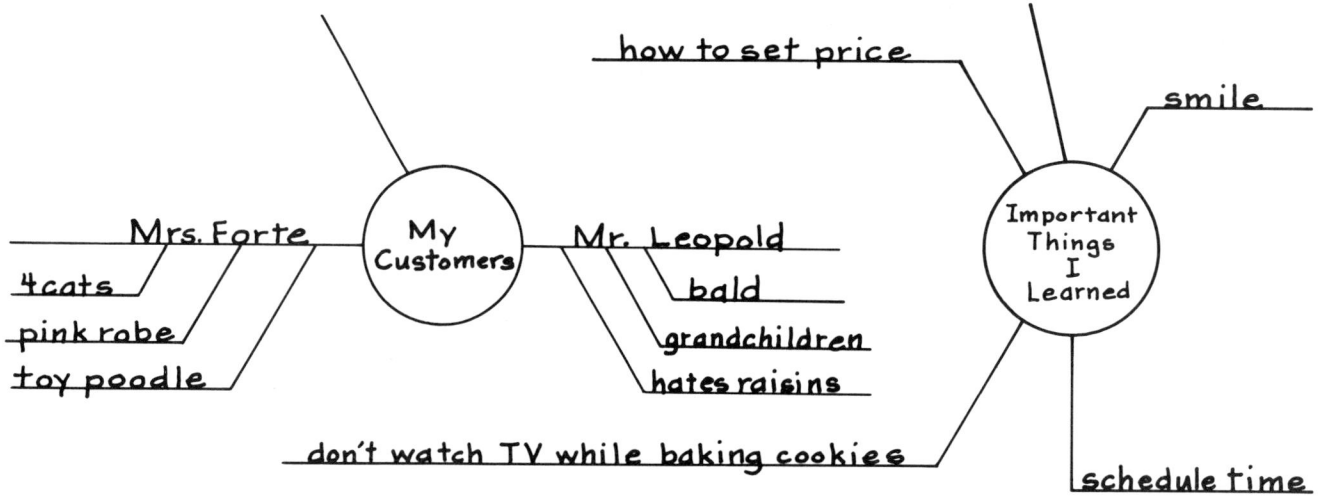

Making Decisions—What to Report

If you try to report on everything that happened during your business career, your presentation will be too long. It might also be boring. Think about the most interesting things you did or learned while running a business. These are the things you might want to share. List two or three ideas here.

a. _____
b. _____
c. _____

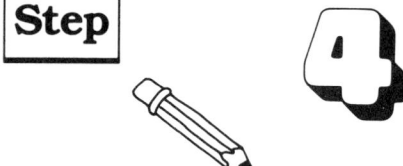

Making Decisions—How to Report

Here are several suggestions for reporting on your business career. Circle the three that you would enjoy doing the most.

poem	song	flannel board	
story	mural	display	mobile
TV newscast	play	puppet show	
game	book	comic book	
newspaper story	(Your own idea)_____		

Rank your choices by putting a 3 by the one you like least. Put a 2 by your second choice. Put a 1 by your first choice.

Step 5 Planning Your Presentation

Plan your presentation carefully. Thinking about these questions may help.

Poem: What part of your career should you write about? How will you organize it? What should the title be? What kind of paper will you write your final copy on?

> Peanut butter, oatmeal
> Chocolate chip and plain.
> Cookies cook in half
>   an hour.
> Waiting's such a pain!
> My friends come to the
>   front door.
> My mother is concerned.
> I say I won't be
>   gone long.
> When I come back,
>   they're burned!

Song: Which of your experiences do you want to sing about? Will you make up a tune or use one you know? Will you need someone else to help you sing or play your song? Will you need instruments for your presentation?

Flannel board story: What story do you want to tell? What scenes do you want to show? What materials will you need? Is a flannel board available at school? Can you practice with the flannel board before your presentation? (*Hint:* Paste sandpaper on your pictures to help them stick to the board.)

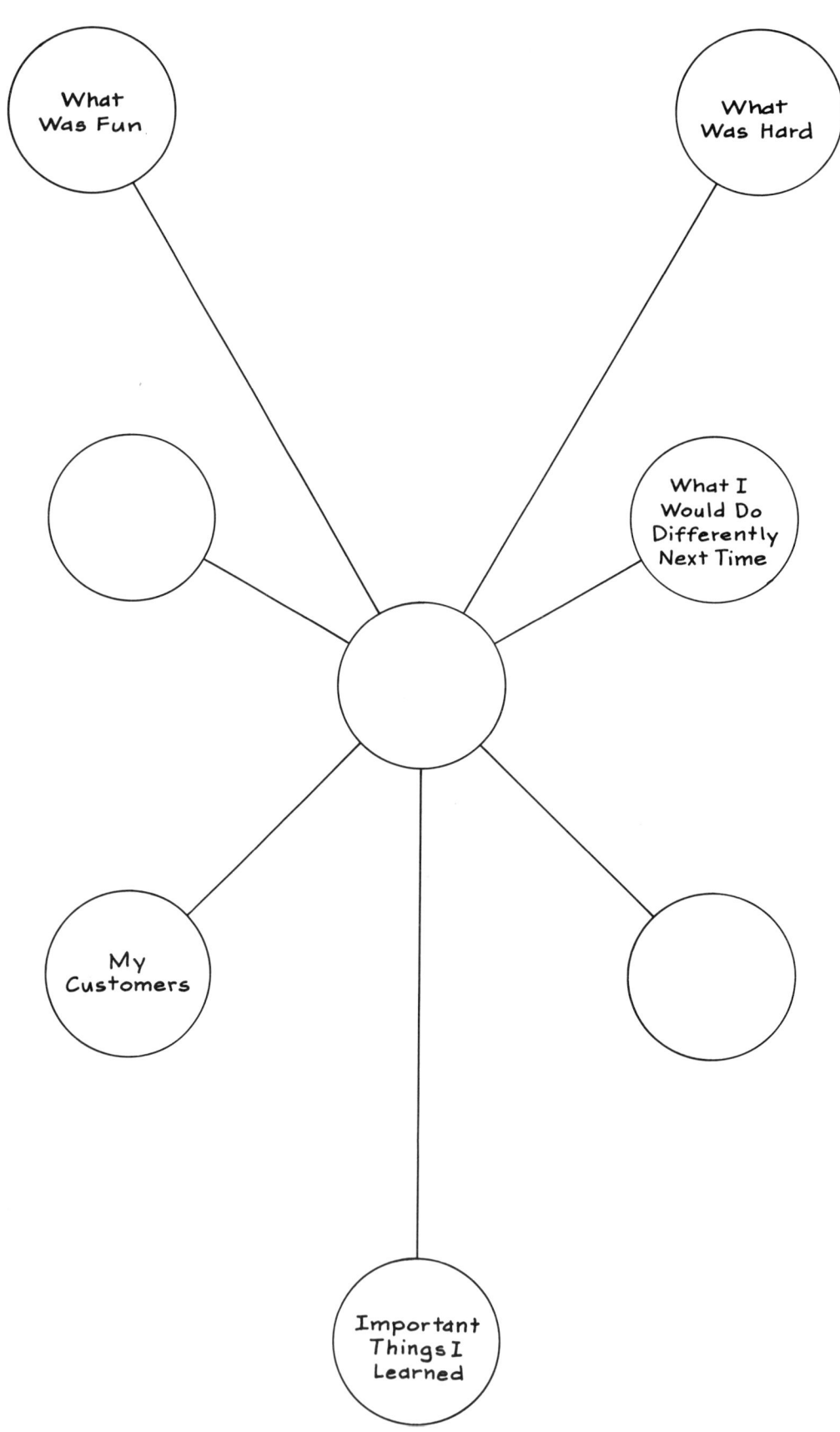

Mural: What parts of your experience do you want to illustrate? How will you arrange these scenes on your mural? What size will your mural be? What materials will you use?

Display: What will you put in your display? (Business records, sample product, service leaflet, etc.) Where can you set it up in your classroom? How will you make it interesting and attractive?

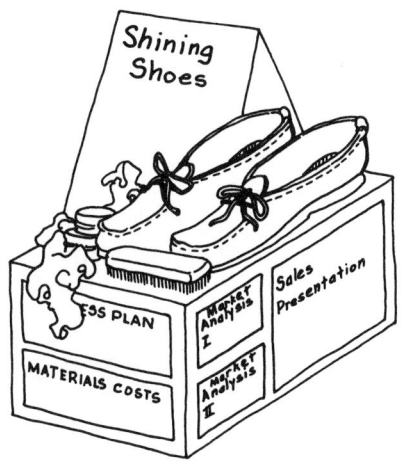

Mobile: What objects, words, or pictures will you hang on your mobile? What materials will you use? Will you need help to make it balance? Where will you hang your mobile in your classroom?

TV newscast: What story do you want to tell? Will you illustrate your story in some way? How should you stand or sit and speak in your newscast? (*Hint:* Watch TV news programs for ideas.)

Play: What part of your business career do you want to act out? How many characters will be in your play? What will each character do and say? Will you perform your play or write it? If you perform your play, who will the actors be?

Puppet show: What story do you want to present? What puppets will you need to make or borrow? Will you need scenery? What will you use for a puppet stage? What will your puppets say and do? Will you need a friend to help you?

Game: What will the object of the game be? (Examples: To start a business or make a profit.) Will it be a board game, card game, or thinking game? What will the rules be? (*Hint:* Keep them simple.) What materials will you need? What is the name of your game?

Book: What story do you want to tell? What will the title be? (Examples: *How to Sell_, The Funniest Customer I Met, Making Something From Junk, My Most Embarrassing Moment, Lessons for a Businessperson*) Will you illustrate your book with pictures? How will you share your book with your class?

Comic book: What parts of your experience do you want to include? What characters will you use? How many pictures will you need to draw? How will you share your book with your class?

Newspaper story: What part of your career would be most interesting to newspaper readers? (*Hint:* Reporters try to tell their readers "who, what, where, when, and why" as they write a story.) What will your headline say? Will you use a picture or illustration with your story?

Step 6

Getting Feedback

Share your presentation with a family member or friend. Then ask these questions.

- Did you understand my presentation?
- Can you think of anything I can change to make it more interesting?

For a written presentation, ask these questions.

- Are all my words spelled correctly?
- Have I used capital letters and periods where I need them?
- Did I put quotation marks around people's words?

For a spoken presentation, ask these questions.

- Did I speak clearly and loudly enough to be heard?
- Did I look out toward you rather than down at my feet?

HOLIDAYS

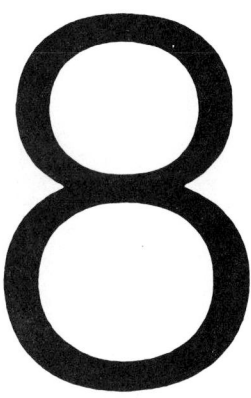

Scope

Seven assignments, each of which will take varying lengths of time, depending on how they are used.

1. Halloween Treats
2. Thanksgiving Turkey Talk
3. A Special Gift
4. Martin Luther King Memorial Speech
5. Community Valentines
6. Arbor Day Tree Study
7. Planning a Festival, Celebration, or Fiesta

Additional Classroom Uses

Math   ■ solving word problems   ■ measuring circumference   ■ comparing

Social Studies   ■ group decision making   ■ researching Martin Luther King   ■ recognizing community helpers

Oral Language   ■ participating in classroom discussions of "sugar highs"   ■ giving feedback

Written Language   ■ story writing   ■ group editing   ■ writing poetry   ■ making vocabulary lists

Fine Arts   ■ applying feedback to an oral presentation   ■ reciting a poem in front of a group   ■ using tree themes in art projects

Study Skills   ■ developing short-term memory

Curriculum Integration

Math   ■ tallying   ■ categorizing   ■ ordering   ■ graphing   ■ writing word problems   ■ ranking

Social Studies   ■ comparing past and present   ■ decision making   ■ identifying community helpers   ■ working in committees

Oral Language   ■ interviewing   ■ brainstorming   ■ eliciting feedback   ■ preparing a speech

Written Language   ■ summarizing   ■ writing a comparison paragraph   ■ organizing a speech   ■ clustering information   ■ writing poetry

Science   ■ identifying   ■ classifying   ■ inferring   ■ collecting evidence   ■ measuring   ■ analyzing observations

Fine Arts   ■ presenting a formal speech   ■ creating a valentine   ■ making a tree model   ■ creating a celebration

Unit Eight

Challenges for GATE Students

- graphing
- predicting
- estimating
- researching
- analyzing
- ordering
- synthesizing
- evaluating
- applying
- hypothesizing
- decision making
- inferring
- categorizing
- writing puns
- taking a census
- setting up learning centers
- designing a playground
- developing leadership skills

Halloween Treats

I. Preassessment Considerations

A. Some of your students may not go trick-or-treating this Halloween. You may need to brainstorm with these students to come up with other things to tally and categorize such as the contents of the refrigerator, a kitchen cupboard, a toy chest, their own closet, or mom's purse.

B. Because this assignment begins on Halloween night for most students, you will want to plan this week's homework schedule accordingly.

C. All your students will enjoy counting and categorizing their treat hordes. Some may need to practice tallying in advance so that they can do this efficiently Halloween night. The children will find that the most challenging parts of the assignment are categorizing and graphing.

II. Integration into the Classroom

A. **Practicing Tallying and Graphing.** Your class can practice tallying almost anything in your classroom from books to crayons. To get into the spirit of the assignment, try tallying colored candies. Give each student a handful and have them list the colors they have on a sheet of paper. Then have them make a tally mark beside the proper color as they sort their candies into color piles. Show children how to group their tally marks into groups of five.

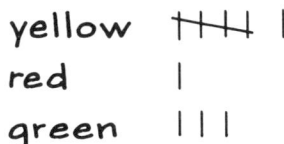

Now ask your students to represent this data on an edible graph by listing their color categories from largest to smallest. Then line up the candies beside their colors. Stress the importance of spacing the candies evenly and lining them up vertically with one just below another so that the graph is easy to read.

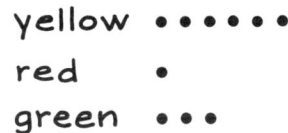

Your students will have no difficulty deciding on the appropriate disposition of their graphs.

B. **Book of Graphs and Questions.** Staple your students' graphs and graph questions into a folder. Encourage children to go through the book during free time to read and answer their friends' questions.

C. **Discussion of "Sugar Highs."** Whereas you may be very aware of the phenomenon sometimes called a "sugar high," particularly on the day after Halloween, your students may not be aware that large amounts of sugar seem to alter behavior in some people. You may want to take time to discuss this subject, possibly asking some of these questions.

- What do you think "sugar highs" are?
- Have you noticed "sugar highs" in someone you know?
- Do you think large amounts of sugar affect you this way?
- When do you think "sugar highs" are likely to occur?
- Can you think of other things that might explain changes in behavior at these times?

III. Extensions for GATE Students

A. More Graphs. Ask your GATE students to use the information they gathered in step 2 to create more complex graphs with each unit representing 5 or 10 treats. They will have to decide how to deal with fractions of 5 or 10.

B. Calendar Calculations. Challenge your GATE students to work out this problem.

Based on the total number of treats you collected, what is the exact day, month, and year you would finish your last treat if you ate only one each day? (Use a calendar to help in figuring this out.)

C. Counting Calories. Begin this activity by explaining that a calorie is a unit used to measure how much energy a food provides. Then present students with an assortment of typical Halloween treats (or have students bring in their own to use), and ask them to group the treats into 500-calorie piles. When they have finished, help them check their estimates using a calorie counting book and information from package labels. If some of your treats are not listed, assist students in making reasonable guesses based on similar items. They may want to rearrange their piles to bring them closer to 500 calories. When you finish, ask each child to choose the 500-calorie pile he or she would most like to eat and to tell why.

D. Ranking Treats. Ask your students to pick three to five criteria used by people in choosing Halloween treats.

Examples; Low cost, good taste, nutritional values, safety, convenience, neatness.

Divide your students into as many groups as you have criteria. Give each group the same five treats, such as an apple, dime, box of raisins, pack of gum, and small candy bar, along with a strip of paper marked like this one.

| Good Taste | 1 | 2 | 3 | 4 | 5 |

Ask each team to rank the five treats according to the criterion on its paper with a rating of 5 being the best and 1 the worst. As each item is ranked, place it over its number.

Students may need special information to rank their treats. You can help by making available wrappers with nutritional and price information; nutrition and calorie guides; newspaper ads with prices of some treats; and most of all, yourself.

E. Creating a Matrix of Treats. When each team has evaluated its treats, combine the rankings to form an evaluation matrix.

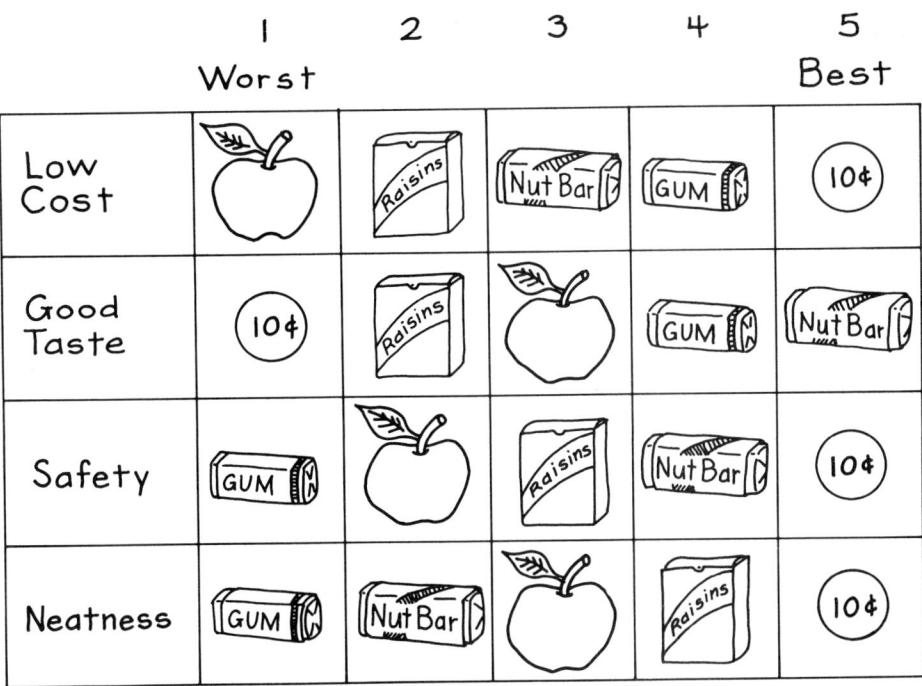

Using the matrix as a guide, ask the group to decide which is the best overall treat. Students may be surprised at the result.

Name

Date Due

Halloween Treats

How many Halloween treats will you collect this year? What kinds of treats will you receive? You'll be able to answer both these questions after this Halloween assignment.

Skills you will develop

- tallying
- categorizing
- grouping by fives
- adding in columns
- ordering
- graphing
- writing questions
- analyzing

What you will need

- your Halloween trick-or-treat goodies
- pencil
- crayons or marking pens

Before you begin: Read the assignment. Plan to do step 1 as soon as you can after trick-or-treating.

Tallying Your Treats

This year after trick-or-treating you will be counting and categorizing your treats, which means sorting them into groups that are alike in some way. In this step you will sort them according to the type of treat they are. The categories are listed on the tally sheet on page 194.

Try this method for counting or tallying your treats: Put them all together in a pile or bowl. Pick up one treat at a time. Decide which category on the tally sheet the treat fits in best. Make a tally mark beside that category. A tally mark looks like a numeral | . Here are the tally marks for three candy bars and two pieces of gum.

candy bars |||
gum pieces ||

Unit Eight

You will find it easier to count your tally marks if you group them by fives. When you come to the fifth item in a category, don't make another tally mark. Instead make a diagonal slash across the four marks you already have: ⊬⊬⊬. Do this for each group of five that you tally. One student's tally for fruit and cookies looked like this.

fruit ⊬⊬⊬

cookies ⊬⊬⊬ ⊬⊬⊬ ||

Here is your tally sheet. Try to categorize and tally each of your treats before you begin eating them.

Halloween Treat Tally Sheet

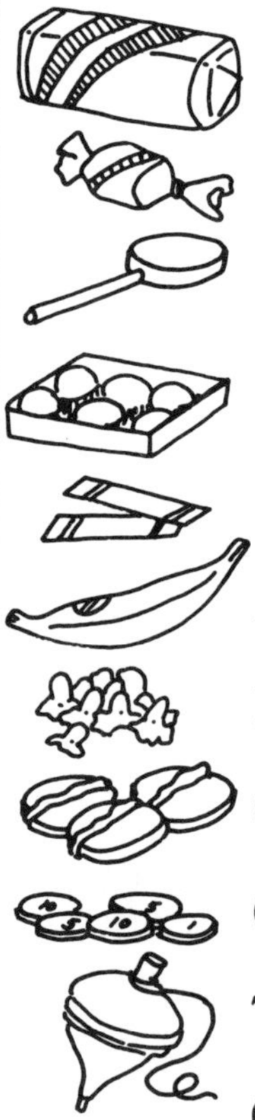

Categories	Totals
Candy bars	
Individual candies	
Candy on a stick	
Candies in packages	
Gum pieces	
Fruit	
Popcorn	
Cookies	
Coins	
Toys	
Others	
	+
GRAND TOTAL	

When you have finished tallying all your treats, count the number you have in each category. This count will go quickly if you count by fives. When you get to the end of your groups of five, add on any other tally marks. Put the total in the box to the right of each category.

Example: Individual candies 𝟝̅ ̅𝟙̅𝟘̅ ̅𝟙̅𝟝̅ ̅𝟚̅𝟘̅ ̅𝟚̅𝟚̅ | 22

(tally: |||| |||| |||| |||| ||)

Figure out your GRAND TOTAL by adding up all the totals in the boxes.

Step 2

Ordering Your Categories

Which category on your tally sheet has the most treats in it? Write the number 1 to the left of that category. Which has the second largest number of treats? Put a number 2 beside that category. Continue ordering your treat categories according to the number of treats until you get to the one with the smallest number. This will be category 12.

If two categories have the same number of treats, you must decide how to order them. Here is an example.

Candy on a stick |||| |||| || | 12

Candy in packages |||| | 5

Gum pieces |||| | 5

Step 3

Graphing Your Treats

Use your tally sheet to fill out the treat graph that follows. First fill in the category names, beginning with your largest category in the space marked 1. List your smallest category in the space marked 12.

For each category, color in one square for each treat of that type that you received. If you came home with 12 bags of popcorn, color in 12 squares beside your popcorn category.

6. popcorn [colored squares]

Use different colors for each category. If you run out of squares, tape another sheet of paper to your graph. Draw in the extra squares you need and color them.

Treat Graph

Categories

1. _____
2. _____
3. _____
4. _____
5. _____
6. _____
7. _____
8. _____
9. _____
10. _____
11. _____
12. _____

Step 4: Making Up Questions about Your Graph

Look over your graph. What things do you notice? Think of two difficult questions your friends could answer using information on your graph. Example: Which category is twice as large as the cookies category?

Write your two questions here.

a. _____

_____

b. _____

_____

Step 5: Categorizing in Other Ways

There are many ways to sort and categorize your treats. Try this one.

Sorting by bite size

Category 1: One-bite treats
(Put all the treats you can eat in one bite in this pile)

Category 2: Two-or-more-bite treats
(Put all the treats that must be eaten in two or more bites in this pile.)

Some items such as coins and toys will not fit in either category.

Think of your own way to sort and categorize your treats. You could sort them by color, cost, flavor, wrapping, size, shape, texture, ingredients, or how long they will keep.

Unit Eight — Halloween Treats

Thanksgiving Turkey Talk

I. Preassessment Considerations

A. If you wait until Thanksgiving week to send this assignment home, students will have only Monday and Tuesday nights to work at home. You can either expect the entire assignment to be done in this time or have students do steps 1 and 2 or 1 through 4 at home and complete the paragraph writing in class. The other alternative is to send the assignment home one week earlier.

B. A few students may have difficulty finding an older person to interview. You might need to help them think of older people they know such as neighbors, church members, or relatives whom they could interview.

C. This assignment will be valuable for all students. The children will find that the most challenging parts are summarizing interview information and synthesizing this information into a well-written paragraph.

II. Integration into the Classroom

A. **Writing as a Class.** Writing a story as a class will give students practice in organizing information and combining simple phrases into complete sentences. Begin by asking your students to think about Thanksgiving from a turkey's point of view. Use a cluster diagram on the chalkboard to organize students' ideas into topics. Then order the topics in terms of what the students think should be written about first, second, and so on. As you work through the topics ask one child at a time to dictate a sentence. Reinforce proper indentation, capitalization, and punctuation while you write their story down on a chalkboard or chart.

B. **Interview Follow-up.** Ask each student to share the most interesting part of their interviews with the rest of the class. Because everyone who did his or her homework should have something to say, this is a perfect time to hear from less verbal students.

C. **Group Editing.** Divide your class into small groups to edit each other's paragraphs. Allow time for each child to read his or her paragraph aloud and for the group to respond with comments and suggestions. You might want to write these questions on the board to guide the discussion.

1. What did you like about my paragraph?
2. Did you understand what I was trying to say?
3. Can you tell what my topic sentence is?
4. Do my supporting sentences fit my topic sentence?
5. Does my concluding sentence tie the paragraph together?
6. How could I improve my paragraph?

Give students time to use this feedback to revise their paragraphs.

D. **Model Paragraphs.** You may want to read aloud or use the overhead projector to display outstanding paragraphs and then discuss with the class what makes them particularly effective.

III. Extensions for GATE Students

A. Creating a Class Book. Ask students with special skills in spelling, grammar, and composition to proofread and edit students' paragraphs. Combine the edited paragraphs to make a class book, preferably typed if you can enlist the aid of a parent volunteer. An artistically gifted student could add simple black-and-white illustrations to the Thanksgiving Book. Your students will feel proud of their work when they share the book with their families.

B. Making Predictions. Using the questions on the interview sheet, have GATE students interview one another about how they imagine they will be celebrating Thanksgiving in the year 2025. They might present some of their predictions to the class by means of a skit, poster, interview, or report. Their presentation should lead to a stimulating discussion involving the entire class.

Name

Date Due

Thanksgiving Turkey Talk

This week you will interview two people about preparing Thanksgiving turkeys both now and in the past.

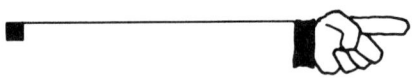

Skills you will develop

- scheduling
- interviewing
- condensing information
- analyzing—comparing
- synthesizing—writing

What you will need

- cooperative adults
- pencil
- paper

Before you begin: Read the assignment. Try to do steps 1 and 2 as soon as you can.

Step 1

Scheduling Two Interviews

Do you think that the way people prepare turkeys for Thanksgiving has changed over the past 50 years? To find out, schedule two interviews. The first should be with someone who remembers preparing Thanksgiving turkeys 30, 40, or even 50 years ago. The second should be with someone who is preparing a turkey for Thanksgiving this year.

When you talk to someone about giving you an interview, set a time to meet together.

First person: Name_____Day_____Time_____

Second person: Name_____Day_____Time_____

Step 2

Interviewing and Condensing Replies

During your interview ask all the questions on the following interview sheet. You will not be able to write down the answers word for word. Instead try to condense the answers you get into a few words.

Unit Eight

201

For example, Mrs. Nilson answered question 1 in this way: "When I was a child, my father and I used to drive out to a farm the weekend before Thanksgiving. There we would get a beautiful, big Tom turkey to take home."

Bob condensed her answer by writing *farm* in the space after that question.

Write a short answer for each question on the sheet.

Interview Sheet

First Person
Preparing turkeys in the past.

1. Where did your family get your Thanksgiving turkey when you were young?

2. How did it come? Alive, freshly killed, or frozen?

3. What had to be done to prepare the turkey for cooking?

4. Was the turkey usually stuffed? If it was, what was in the stuffing?

5. How was the turkey cooked?

6. Who usually carved the turkey?

7. Who usually came to eat the turkey?

Second Person
Preparing turkeys today.

1. Where will you get your Thanksgiving turkey this week?

2. How will it come? Alive, freshly killed, or frozen?

3. What will you have to do to prepare the turkey for cooking?

4. Will you stuff the turkey? If so, what will be in your stuffing?

5. How will you cook the turkey?

6. Who will carve the turkey?

7. Who will be eating the turkey with you this year?

Step 3: Analyzing Your Interview Sheet

Look carefully at both answers to each question. If the answers match, or seem to be about the same, draw a line between them. Here is an example.

6. Who usually carved the turkey?   6. Who will carve the turkey?

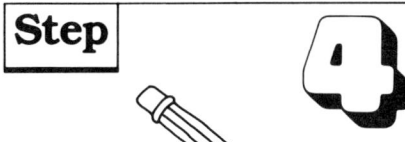

If the answers are different, draw a circle around each one.

5. How was the turkey cooked?   5. How will you cook the turkey?

Step 4: Choosing a Topic for a Paragraph

Now you are ready to plan a paragraph. To begin, which of these topics fit your interview answers best? Circle your choice.

Topic 1: Thanksgiving today is a lot like it used to be.
Topic 2: Thanksgiving today is different in some ways than it used to be.
Topic 3: Thanksgiving has changed in many ways since the past.

Step 5: Planning a Paragraph

The Paragraph Planning Chart on page 205 will help you plan a well-written paragraph.

Topic Sentence: A good paragraph has three parts. The first is a topic sentence. This sentence tells what the paragraph is about. Everything else in your paragraph should connect to your topic sentence.

Use the topic you circled in step 4 to help you think of a topic sentence. Write it in the space on the chart marked "Topic Sentence." Here are two examples to get you started.

1. Preparing a turkey for Thanksgiving was harder in the past than it is now.
2. Thanksgiving hasn't changed much in our family.

Supporting Sentences: The second part of a paragraph is the information that supports or explains your topic sentence. Use the information on your interview sheet to write three sentences to support your topic sentence. Here are some examples.

1. My grandmother used to get a live turkey every year.
2. She had to kill it, pull out the feathers and clean out the insides.
3. My mother buys a frozen turkey that is ready to cook.

Concluding Sentences: The third part of a paragraph is the concluding sentence. This sentence ties the paragraph together in some way. Your concluding sentence might tell how you feel about what you have written. You may want to say why you wrote about these things. Or you may want to sum up your paragraph in some other ways. Here are examples to get you thinking.

1. I'm glad Thanksgiving has not changed very much.
2. Even though cooking a turkey is easier today, getting together to eat it is just as much fun as it used to be.

Paragraph Planning Chart

Topic Sentence:

Write a sentence telling what your paragraph is about. Everything else should connect to this sentence. Example: "I learned some surprising things about preparing a turkey these days."

_____
_____
_____
_____

Supporting Sentences:

Support your topic sentence by writing three things about your topic sentence. Example: "It takes two days for a frozen turkey to thaw."

a. _____
_____

b. _____
_____

c. _____
_____

Concluding Sentence:

In your last sentence, tie everything together in some way. Example: "This year I will enjoy eating turkey more than ever."

_____
_____
_____
_____
_____

Step 6: Synthesizing by Writing a Paragraph

Before you go on to write your paragraph, check these things. If you are not sure you can answer "yes" to each question, show your planning chart to someone else and ask the same questions. That person may be able to help you improve your ideas before you write your final paragraph.

1. Does your topic sentence tell what the paragraph is about?
2. Does each of your supporting ideas help explain the topic sentence in some way?
3. Does your concluding sentence fit with the other ideas in your paragraph?

Write your final paragraph on a clean sheet of paper. When you finish it should look something like this:

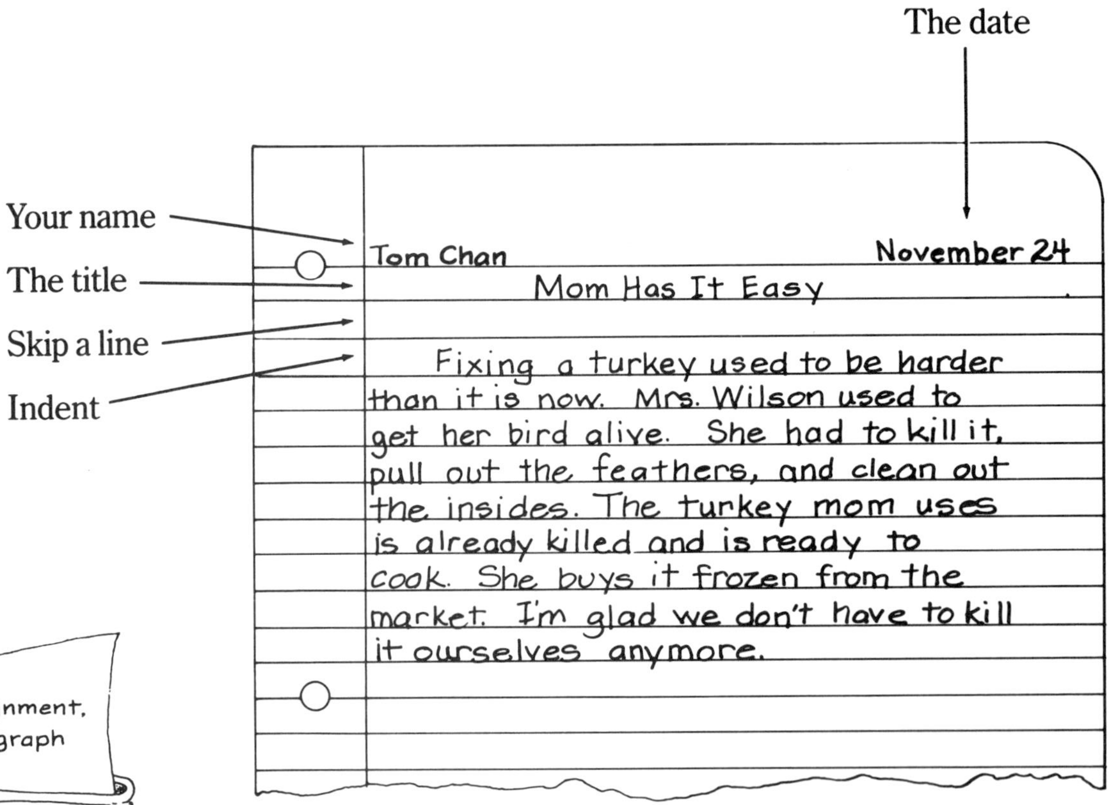

- Your name → Tom Chan
- The date → November 24
- The title → Mom Has It Easy
- Skip a line
- Indent →

Fixing a turkey used to be harder than it is now. Mrs. Wilson used to get her bird alive. She had to kill it, pull out the feathers, and clean out the insides. The turkey mom uses is already killed and is ready to cook. She buys it frozen from the market. I'm glad we don't have to kill it ourselves anymore.

Bring Back: assignment, paragraph

A Special Gift

I. Preassessment Considerations

    A. This assignment could be used anytime during the year, but because it emphasizes giving, it is ideal for the Christmas/Hanukkah season. The nonsectarian nature of the assignment should make its use during this season noncontroversial.

    B. The assignment does not require that gifts be given to specific people such as parents or guardians. If this is your intention, be sure to tell your students. Students should know the recipients of their gifts well in order to think of uniquely suitable presents for them.

    C. The children will find that the most challenging parts of this assignment are brainstorming gift ideas and following up on gift certificates.

II. Integration into the Classroom

    A. Discussion on Giving. During the holiday season, gift giving traditions differ from family to family and from country to country. You might share some different national traditions with your students and ask them to talk about their family traditions. Questions like these will help focus the ensuing discussion on the assignment.

- Why do we give gifts?
- What problems do children have in giving gifts?
- Do gifts have to cost money?
- What kinds of gifts do not cost money?

    B. Class Gift Certificate. Before you send the assignment home, go through the process of creating a gift certificate in class. Begin by selecting a person whom the entire class would like to honor with a gift; the receiver could be a valued volunteer, the school custodian, or last year's teacher, for example. When you have finished brainstorming and ranking gift ideas, have one student make up a gift certificate on behalf of the class and deliver it. Set a date when the class will follow through on its promise, and make certain that each student is clear about his or her responsibility to complete the gift.

    C. Sharing Gift Ideas. Some students may have trouble thinking up good gift ideas until they hear others talk about their plans. It may help to set aside time during the week for the sharing of ideas.

III. Extensions for GATE Students

    A. Ranking Other Activities. Suggest to your GATE students that they adapt the ranking technique in this assignment to other areas. They could, for example, rank free time or recess activities, topics for a report, or ideas for a project. Here is how a ranking of free classtime activities might look.

Activity	Easiest to Set Up		Most Fun		Total
Reading a book		+		=	
Playing a math game		+		=	
Doing an art project		+		=	
Cleaning desk		+		=	
Staring at ceiling		+		=	

(Rank from 1 to 5, with 5 the top rating.)

B. **Gift Hypotheses.** Present your GATE students with several gift certificates you have made for a variety of people. The students' task is to come up with plausible hypotheses about the type of person you had in mind when designing each gift.

IV. Applying This Assignment to Your Classroom Program

A. The brainstorming and ranking process used in this assignment can be used in planning a wide variety of classroom activities, from physical education activities to science projects.

B. In your reading program you can challenge students to think of appropriate gifts for fictional characters, which will increase students' sensitivity to the characters they meet in literature. What would be the best gifts for Flat Stanley, Wilbur the pig, Amelia Bedelia, etc.? If students have difficulty coming up with good ideas, it may be that the characters they are dealing with are poorly drawn.

Name

Date Due

A Special Gift

Get into the spirit of the holiday season by thinking of a special gift for a very special person.

Skills you will develop

- brainstorming
- making decisions
- analyzing—ranking
- getting feedback
- revising
- decorating

What you will need

- someone to brainstorm with
- pencil
- paper
- crayons or marking pens

Before you begin: Read steps 1 through 6.

Brainstorming About Someone Special

Think of someone special in your life—someone to whom you would like to give a special gift this holiday season. You might choose a parent, relative, teacher, or good friend.

Find someone who knows your special person. Sit down together for a few minutes of brainstorming about what your special person likes. Here is what two people wrote down while they brainstormed about what Aunt Margaret likes.

Aunt Margaret

mystery books
rings   rock music
    karate   compliments   pink
eating   jewelry   wigs
    clothes   diamonds
lavender gloves   hats   roller skating
    traveling   ice cream
attention   riding a bike
    valentines   singing and dancing

Unit Eight

Brainstorming is a way of coming up with a lot of ideas in a short time. When people brainstorm they write down every idea they think of. No thoughts are rejected because they seem silly or strange. Even strange ideas sometimes lead to new and better ideas.

Write the name of your special person at the top of a piece of blank paper. As you and your fellow brainstormer think of things your special person likes, write them down.

Step 3: Making Decisions About What to Give

For most people the best gift is a gift of yourself. This means doing something for a person, something you know that person would like. Such a gift costs nothing but your time.

Look over your brainstorming sheet. Circle any items that make you think of something you can do for your special person. Be creative. If you don't find at least four things to circle, do some more brainstorming.

Here are four gift ideas for Aunt Margaret to get you thinking.

Gift of Yourself Ideas—Aunt Margaret

a. Glue her travel pictures into an album for her.
b. Give her a compliment every day for a week.
c. Help her organize her hats and clothes.
d. Take her on a special bike ride.

Write four gift ideas for your special person in the following spaces.

Gift of Yourself Ideas—A Special Person

a. _____

b. _____

c. _____

d. _____

Step 3

Ranking Your Gift Ideas

Which gift should you give? The numbered statements below will help you rank your gift ideas. Start with the first idea marked *a*. Decide which statement fits this idea best. Write that number in the box to the left of this gift idea. When you have ranked all four ideas, each box should have a different number in it.

| 1 | The least fun for me to do.
| 2 | I wouldn't mind doing this.
| 3 | Better than 1 and 2, but not what I would like doing best.
| 4 | I would enjoy doing this the most.

Now try ranking your gift ideas in another way. This time write the number that best fits each gift idea in the triangle to the left of each idea. Here are the statements to match to your gift ideas.

 My special person would enjoy this least.

 My special person would like this.

 Better than 1 and 2, but not what my special person would like most.

 My special person would enjoy this most of all.

Finish ranking your gift ideas by adding the number in the box to the number in the triangle. Write the total in the circle.

$$\square + \triangle = \bigcirc$$

The best gift for you to give is probably the one with the largest total in the circle.

Step 4: Making a Rough Draft of Your Gift Certificate

Use this form to make a rough draft of a gift certificate for your special person.

Write the name of your special person here.

Write what you plan to do. Use a complete sentence starting with "I will_____."

Tell when you plan to do this.

Sign your name here.

Gift Certificate—Rough Draft

To_____

My special gift_____

_____

_____

_____

To be done_____

From_____

Step 5: Getting Feedback

Show your rough draft to an adult and ask these questions.

- Do you understand what I plan to do?
- Is my spelling correct?
- Have I used capital letters and periods where I should?

Step 6: Revising and Decorating Your Certificate

Use your feedback to revise and improve your rough draft. Then with your best printing fill out the final gift certificate on the next page. When you are finished writing, decorate the certificate using crayons or marking pens.

It is up to you to decide when you want to give your gift certificate to your special person.

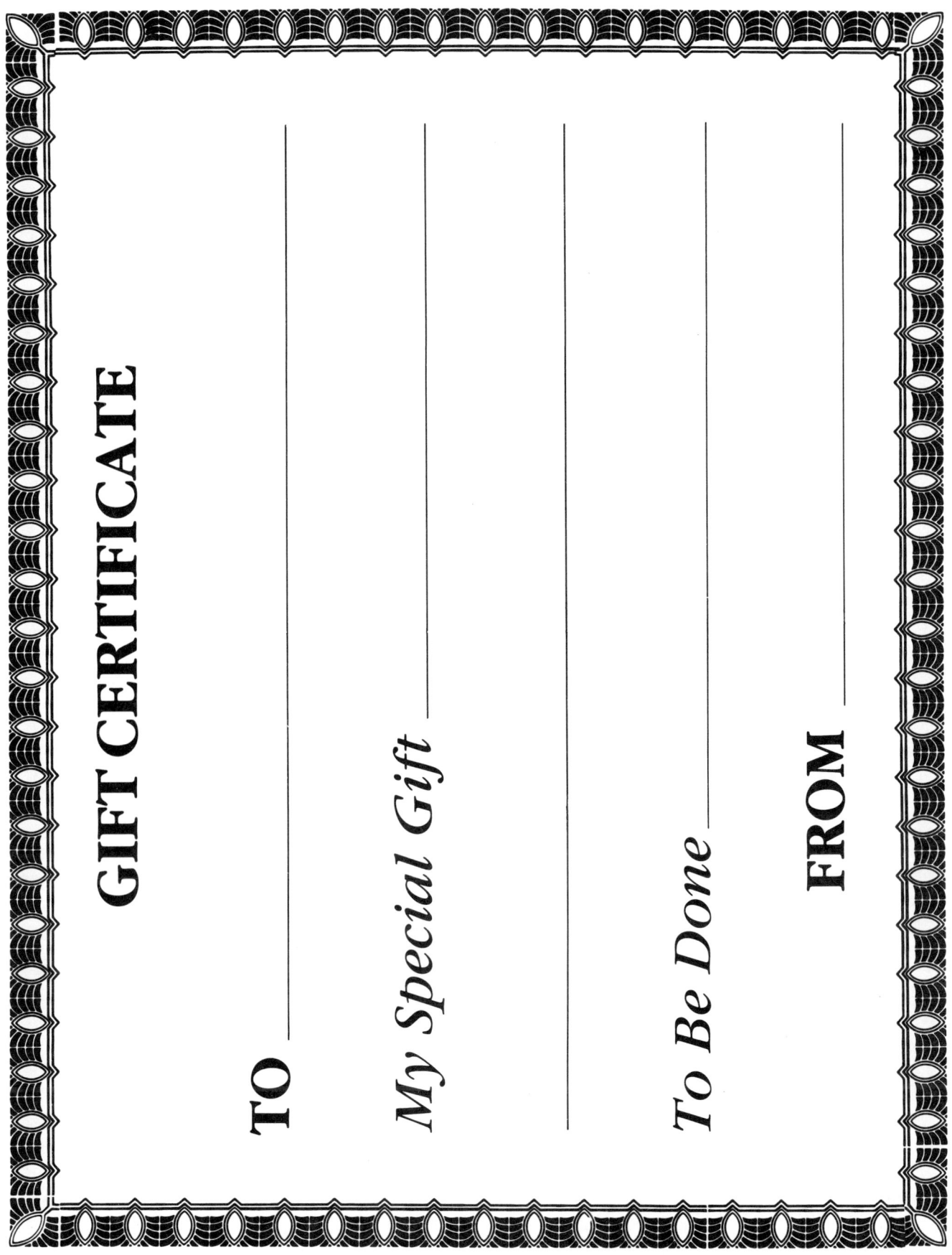

Martin Luther King Memorial Speech

I. Preassessment Considerations

A. Because Martin Luther King Day is celebrated in the middle of January, you may want to start planning a memorial program before the December holidays. This could take the form of an all-school assembly, a grade level presentation, a parents' night program, or a community celebration. Whatever you decide, the value of this assignment will be greatly enhanced if the final presentation of speeches is made to a group larger than your class.

B. This assignment may prove difficult for students with limited parental help, because it requires some support and feedback from home. Such children might make their contribution to the program in other ways, such as by creating artwork, collecting background information on King, serving refreshments, or producing a printed program.

C. The assignment can be completed in one week, but the speeches may be more polished if children have two weeks to prepare. You might divide the assignment by sending home the material through step 2 the first week and then steps 3 through 6 the following week.

D. Almost every child will be nervous about making a speech. You will have to judge whether this assignment is too demanding for some of your students. The children will find that the most challenging aspects are (1) organizing supporting information, (2) condensing information, and (3) speaking in front of a group.

II. Integration into the Classroom

A. **Introducing Martin Luther King.** This assignment will have more meaning for students the more they know about Martin Luther King's life and legacy. Experience has shown the wisdom of reserving books, tapes, films, and records concerning King well in advance.

B. **Brainstorming Dream Ideas.** Students may do a better job of selecting speech topics if you do some brainstorming in class before you send the assignment home. You might guide the discussion by asking questions that lead from students' own lives to broader concerns.

Examples: "What do you dream about doing in your own lives? What changes would you like to see in our school? What changes can you dream of that would improve our community? state? nation? world?"

C. **Planning a Speech in Class.** Because the process of planning a speech will be new to most students, you may want to model it in class using a topic suggested by students. Using the speech planning chart as a guide, write the opening, main points, and closing as a group.

D. **Writing Speech Notes.** Many children will find condensing their speech notes difficult. You may be able to help by doing step 3 of the assignment in class. Use one student's speech planning chart as an example, and go through the condensing process together. Then have students work in pairs, where they will decide together how to reduce their own sentences to just a few words. When they have finished, you may want to have them cut out their notes and glue them to heavier paper. These notes can go home with steps 4 through 6 for practice and feedback.

E. **Classroom Critiquing.** Your speakers will benefit greatly from having an opportunity to practice their speeches in front of a group. At the same time, all your students may sharpen their listening and observation skills by critiquing each speech. Arrange your room in formal audience style if possible, and give each student several feedback sheets like the one that follows. Explain the rating system and ask students to wait until the speech is finished to write down their ratings.

F. **Feedback Groups.** When all the speakers have finished, divide the class into two or three feedback groups. The feedback sheets will help students remember and critique each speech. Suggest that each critique begin with positive statements and then move on to areas that need improvement.

Examples: "You spoke loudly and clearly and stood up straight. I loved your ending. I suggest that you look at your audience more and slow down."

"I gave you all 4s except for item c, because I could barely hear you."

Encourage your speakers to use this feedback to improve their final presentations.

G. **Preparing to Go Onstage.** Everyone will be nervous about speaking, but you can help students relax by telling them to visualize their speeches in advance. If possible, visit the scene of the final presentations. Let students see where they will sit, walk, and stand to speak. One student might walk on and off stage as an example. Then ask students to close their eyes and take three deep breaths, letting the air out slowly. In a soft, soothing voice help them picture each step.

"Picture yourself sitting in your chair. Now it is your turn to speak. You are walking . . . standing in front of the audience . . . speaking loudly and clearly. People are applauding as you begin walking back to your seat. Now you sit down feeling really proud of yourself."

H. **Speech Follow-up.** After the presentations encourage students to share their feelings before they make their speeches. (For example, they may have cold hands, nervous stomachs, hot ears, etc.) At the same time be sure to recognize students who used feedback to improve their speeches.

IV. Applying This Assignment to Your Classroom Program

A. You may want to use the feedback sheets and group critiques for other presentations such as oral book reports and show and tell. The quality of such presentations will improve dramatically as students become familiar with the five criteria and learn what areas they need to work on.

B. The habit of mental rehearsal is common to peak performers in all fields, from athletics to teaching and business. Top performers visualize themselves doing important tasks in advance, considering the many things that might come up and how they will react. You can help students develop this habit of mental rehearsal by encouraging them to visualize themselves doing difficult activities in advance. This might be especially useful before an interview, a performance, a visit with the principal, or an athletic contest.

Feedback Sheet

Here are five things to be looking and listening for with each speaker.

a. Stands straight
b. Looks calm
c. Speaks loudly
d. Speaks slowly and clearly
e. Looks at the audience

Ratings
1. Needs a lot of work
2. Needs some work
3. Pretty good
4. Very good

Rate how well the speaker does on each skill by writing a number from 1 to 4 beside each letter. Wait until the speaker is done before you write.

Speaker's name _____   Speaker's name _____

a.   a.
b.   b.
c.   c.
d.   d.
e.   e.

Speaker's name _____   Speaker's name _____

a.   a.
b.   b.
c.   c.
d.   d.
e.   e.

Speaker's name _____   Speaker's name _____

a.   a.
b.   b.
c.   c.
d.   d.
e.   e.

Name

Date Due

Martin Luther King Memorial Speech

Martin Luther King Jr. was one of America's great civil rights leaders. This week you will make a speech in honor of his memory.

Skills you will develop

- choosing a speech topic
- planning a speech
- making speech notes
- rehearsing a speech
- getting feedback
- making a speech

What you will need

- pencil
- scissors
- large mirror

When Martin Luther King Jr. was growing up he dreamed of becoming a great speaker. He wanted to make fiery speeches to help bring about a better life for black Americans. In school he worked hard to "get the big words" he wanted for his speeches. He practiced speaking in front of groups whenever he could.

The skill Martin Luther King developed as a speaker helped him become a great leader. King knew how to talk to people. He could get people to listen to his ideas. And he could win their support in his struggle for equal rights for blacks.

During his lifetime King made thousands of speeches. One speech, however, is remembered more than any other. King made it on August 28, 1963. That day 250,000 people poured into Washington, D.C., from all over the nation. They had come to protest unfair treatment given to many black Americans.

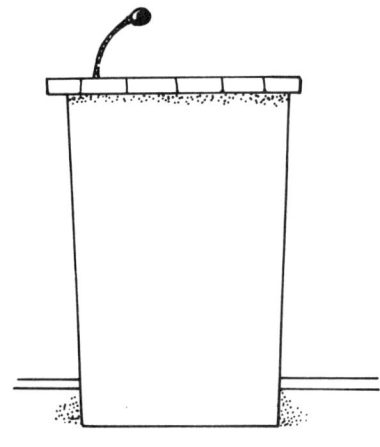

When King looked out on that huge sea of faces he saw blacks and whites, young and old, rich and poor. He wanted to touch their hearts, to give them hope to keep on fighting for equal rights. Even more, King wanted to win the support of the millions who would hear him talk on radio and television.

"I have a dream," said King in his rich, deep voice. "I have a dream that my four little children will one day live in a nation where they will not be judged by the color of their skin." He dreamed of a time when "little black boys and black girls will be able to join hands with little white boys and white girls and walk together as sisters and brothers." King dreamed of a country free from hate and prejudice. He dreamed that someday Americans of all colors and religions "will be able to join hands and sing in the words of the old Negro spiritual, 'Free at last! Free at last! Thank God Almighty, we are free at last'."

This week you will be following in Martin Luther King's footsteps by planning and making a short speech. In honor of his memory your speech should begin with his words "I have a dream."

Choosing a Topic

The topic of your speech should be a special dream of your own. Your dream can be for yourself, your family, school, community, or country. Here are some examples of topics.

- I have a dream that I will grow up to become the first woman president.
- I have a dream that the park in our neighborhood will be cleaned up so that children can play there safely.
- I have a dream that the children in our school will learn to solve their problems by talking instead of fighting.

If you have trouble choosing a topic, talk over your ideas with someone.

Planning Your Speech

Good speakers plan their talks in advance. This does not mean you must write out every word. It does mean that you must decide what you want to say and in what order you will say it.

A speech can be divided into three parts: the opening, the main points, and the closing. The speech planning chart on the next two pages will help you plan each part of your talk.

Speech Planning Chart

Part 1: The Opening A good opening tells people what you are going to talk about. It also catches their interest so that they want to hear more. Use the topic you chose in step 1 to finish this opening.

I have a dream that _____

_____

_____

Part 2: The Main Points Here are some of the main points you may want to make about your dream. If you have other points to make, write them down as well. Use the other side of this sheet if you need more space.

Point 1: My dream is important to me because _____

_____

Point 2: My dream is important to my _____

(parents, class, school, neighborhood, friends, country)

because _____

_____

Point 3: If my dream came true _____

_____

_____

Point 4: _____

_____

_____

Part 3: The Closing The last words of your speech should give your listeners something to think about. Here are some examples of closings.

- I think I would make a good president. I hope someday you will vote for me.
- Would you join me in a clean-up project? Together we can make my dream of a clean, safe park come true.
- If we all begin using our brains instead of our fists to settle fights, our school will be a better and safer place.

Write your closing here. _____
_____
_____
_____

Step 3 Making Speech Notes

Good speakers don't try to memorize their speeches. A talk sounds more natural if it is not memorized word for word. Many speakers do make speech notes for themselves. These notes remind them of what they planned to say. Usually they put these notes on cards. If they get stuck, a quick look at their cards reminds them what to talk about next.

You should be able to get all your notes for your speech on this card. Use just enough words on each line to remind you about what to say next. Here are examples of how the closings in step 3 might be shortened for speech notes.

- Good president. Vote for me.
- Clean-up project. Clean, safe park.
- Use brains, not fists.

Be sure to write neatly and clearly. When you are finished, cut out your card.

"I Have a Dream" Speech Notes

Opening _____
Main points

1. _____
2. _____
3. _____
4. _____
5. _____

Closing _____

Step 4: Rehearsing Your Speech

Stand in front of a large mirror and practice your speech. Then ask yourself these questions. Practice until you can answer *yes* to all of them.

(To rehearse means to practice for a performance.)

a. Did I stand up straight?
b. Did I look calm with no wiggling and squirming?
c. Did I speak loudly enough to be heard?
d. Did I speak slowly and clearly so that I could be understood?
e. Did I look out toward my audience and not down at my notes most of the time?

Step 5: Getting Feedback

Ask a friend or parent to listen to your speech. Pretend that you are in front of your class speaking. Ask that person all five questions from step 5. How many *yes* answers did you get? If you got some *no* answers, use this feedback to improve your speech.

Step 6: Making Your Speech

Now you are ready to make your speech in front of your class. You may feel nervous. Most speakers do at first. These tips may help you.

a. Take your notes with you. They can be a lifesaver if your mind goes blank. Look at them quickly to find out what to say next.
b. Just before you begin, take a deep breath. Hold it. Then let it out slowly. This should help you relax.
c. If you don't know what to do with your hands, use them both to hold your notes. This is better than twisting a button or scratching your ear while you speak.
d. You may find it hard to look at your audience. If so, look at the wall behind your listeners and not down at your feet or notes.
e. Smile. This will make everyone feel better.

Community Valentines

I. Preassessment Considerations

A. You may want to monitor students' choices of community helpers to make sure that a variety of people are recognized.

B. Students will enjoy this assignment. The children will find that the most challenging parts are (1) writing valentine poems, (2) creating aesthetically pleasing cards, and (3) following through on delivery.

II. Integration into the Classroom

A. **Valentine Memory Game.** For this game you will need a large ball of yarn and a place where children can sit in a circle. You might start the game by telling whom you plan to send a valentine card to and why, and then tossing the ball of yarn to a student while you keep hold of the end yourself. The yarn ball will travel more easily if you unwind some yarn before throwing or rolling it.

The child receiving the yarn reveals his or her choice for a community valentine, takes a firm grip on the yarn, and then tosses the ball to someone else.

Examples: "I am sending a valentine to Mrs. White, because she helps me find good books in the library."

"I'm making a valentine for Officer Keller, because he helped my brother find his lost bike."

Continue this way until every child has had a chance to state his or her valentine and is holding onto the yarn. The last child then reverses the process, sending the ball back to where it came from while repeating that student's valentine choice and reason.

Example: "Kerry is sending a valentine to the people who pick up the trash in her building, because without them there would be a big mess."

The child receiving the ball should wind up the slack while trying to remember the choice of the next student. The game is finished when all the yarn has been rewound. Students will have an easier time remembering each other's choices if you warn them in advance to pay close attention to what each person says.

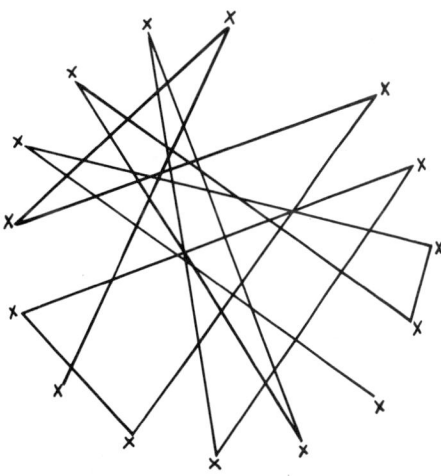

B. Class Valentine. With your class, choose a school staff worker or volunteer to send a valentine to. Use the chalkboard to create a cluster diagram on that person.

Write a valentine poem as a class, and then set one or two students to work at designing the card while the rest of the class brainstorms on ways to deliver the card.

C. Writing Valentine Poems. Your students will feel more comfortable writing poems if they practice doing so in class. Their practice poems could be on any subject. Here are some approaches that have been used successfully with students.

   1. *Rhyming Poems.* Traditional valentine cards used short, singsong rhymes. These ideas may help children think of their own rhymes.
      a. Look for curious combinations of rhyming words.
         frog/smog   slime/dime   sly/fly   brook/snook
      b. Explore half-rhymes.
         cup/cop   roof/truth   moon/mean
      c. Pair students to write couplets.
         First child: "I gulped down a 7-Up."
         Second child: "My tummy answered with a hiccup."
      d. Put new words to common rhymes found in songs, commercials, jingles, or jump-rope chants.
   2. *Repetitive Poems.* Have students finish these repetitive poems with a variation at the end.

      I like_____.   Mother always_____.
      You do_____.   Mother always_____.
      I like_____.   Mother always_____.
      You do_____.   She never_____.
      _____I don't like.
      _____You don't do.

   3. *Alliterative Poems.* Challenge students to use the same initial sound for as many words as possible in a poem. Example:

      To my pop, the policeman
      Who prowls Potrero Hill.
      He peeks, prowls, and pries.
      He protects public property
      And preserves the peace at home.

   4. *Metaphorical Poems.* Encourage students to connect their favorite people with favorite things. Example:

      Grandma B.
      comforter of feathered softness
      cookie jar of sweetness
      and a lap full of hugs.

D. Card Design. Most children will overdo their cards by filling every square inch with some design element and using every color in their crayon boxes. Time spent in class discussing card design will pay off in more attractive valentines. You may want to put particular emphasis on the discrete use of just a few colors and the importance of negative or empty space. Examples of well-designed cards made by children will help you make your points.

E. Valentine Delivery. Your students will be able to brainstorm several clever ways to deliver their cards. For those who plan to mail their cards, Addressing an Envelope in Unit 9 will prove helpful. You may want to follow up to make sure that deliveries are carried out.

F. Brown Bag Helpers Lunch. You can honor the children's community helpers by inviting them to a brown-bag lunch. If you keep it simple, the occasion will carry itself. Have students issue the invitations and bring two bag lunches that day, one for themselves and one for their helpers. A parent volunteer might be asked to provide a drink. Students can help by rearranging the room and making decorations.

Your luncheon program could consist of each child reading his or her valentine and presenting it to the helper. Don't forget to invite a reporter from the local newspaper to cover this event.

III. Extensions for GATE Students

A. Valentine Learning Center. Your GATE students can create a simple learning center by collecting a wide variety of valentine cards. The task at this center is for students to find ways of sorting the cards into two or more categories. Post a sheet for students to record their ideas. Entries might look something like this.

Encourage each student to find a way of categorizing cards that has not been done by someone else. As they search for new approaches their categories will become more subtle and complex.

B. Student Editors. Gifted writers can help students who are having trouble writing their valentine poems by acting as editors or ghost writers.

C. Punning. Challenge your GATE students to collect valentine puns and then create more of their own. Examples:

"To a cool cat . . . you're purrfect!"

"Valentine! You're acute triangle."

Name

Date Due

Community Valentines

Have you ever sent a valentine to a fire fighter or a librarian? You might this Valentine's Day.

Skills you will develop

- analyzing
- clustering
- synthesizing—writing poetry
- creating a valentine card
- following through

What you will need

- pencil
- crayons or marking pens
- paper
- large envelope
- materials for your valentine
- glue or paste

Before you begin: Read steps 1 through 5.

Choosing a Valentine in Your Community

Here is a list of some of the community helpers whom you may know.

- bus driver
- police officer
- mail carrier
- fire fighter
- garbage collector
- street sweeper
- coach
- paramedic
- librarian
- crossing guard
- social worker
- (your own idea)

Draw a red heart beside the three helpers you would most like to send a valentine to. Put two hearts by your favorite.

Clustering Information

The cluster diagram on page 228 will help you analyze what your favorite helper does. Write the name of your favorite helper in the center if you know it. If you don't, write in the person's job.

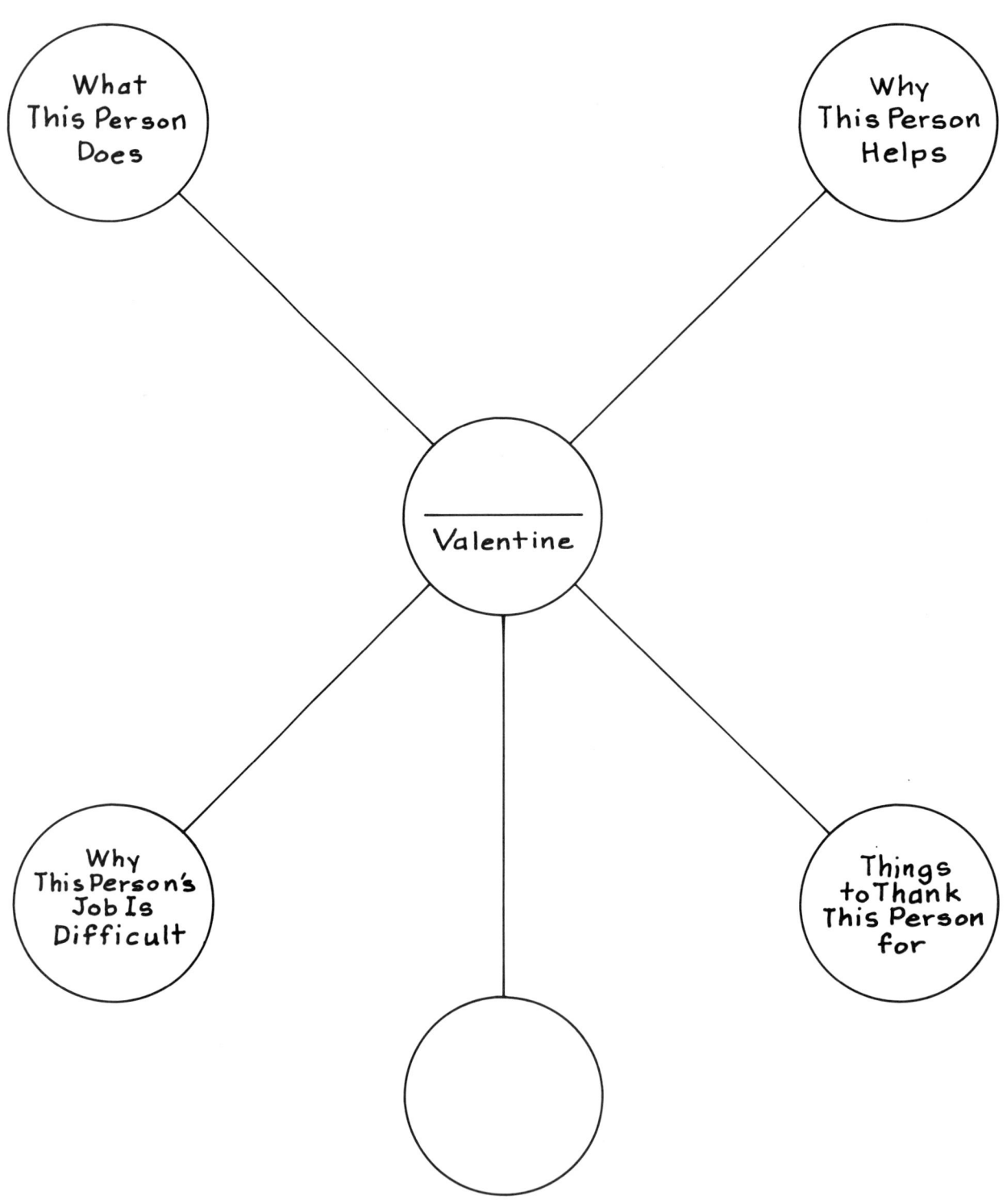

Step 3: Writing a Valentine Poem

Use scratch paper and a pencil to write a valentine poem about your choice in step 2. Your cluster should give you some ideas. The best poem is one that makes your valentine person feel special and appreciated. Here are some examples to get you thinking.

You're the librarian who helps me find
Books that entertain my mind.
Please say you'll be my valentine.

Some kids like to play robbers,
Some kids like to play cops.
This kid's sending you a valentine
Because I think you're tops.

Picking up trash can't be fun.
You must be tired when your day is done.
So I am making this card for you
To cheer you up when your work is through.

The Fire Fighters of Firehouse 5 are

V ery brave.
A lways ready.
L ast to leave a fire.
E ager to help.
N ice to visit.
T errific drivers.
I nteresting to talk to.
N eat and clean.
E asy to like.

Write your finished poem here. If you need more space, use the back of this sheet.

_____
_____
_____
_____

Step 4: Creating a Valentine Card

To make your valentine, you will need blank paper, an envelope, and marking pens. You may also want to decorate your card with scraps and materials from around the house. Here are some ideas of things to use.

> Foil, lace, fabric scraps, pictures or letters from magazines, doilies, stickers, glitter, yarn, beads, junk jewelry, ribbons, old valentine cards, wrapping paper, wallpaper scraps, feathers.

Begin your card by deciding how to cut or fold your paper so it will fit in the envelope.

Next decide where your poem will go on the card. You may want to write it in pencil first to be sure it fits. Then go over the pencil with marking pen. At the end of the poem write your name and age.

Finally, decorate your card. You may want to use marking pens alone. You can also glue on some of the materials you have gathered in an interesting or pleasing way. Be sure you let the glue dry before you put the card in the envelope.

Step 5: Following Through—Delivering Your Card

Here are some ways to deliver a valentine. You may think of more.

- Mail it. Ask a grownup to help you find the address and a stamp.
- Deliver it to the person yourself.
- Leave it where it cannot be missed, like on a garbage can or the bus driver's seat.

How do you plan to deliver your valentine?_____

Arbor Day Tree Study

I. Preassessment Considerations

A. Arbor Day falls in March, April, or May in most states. Check your calendar to find out when it is celebrated in your area. At this time of year most trees are leafing out, but there may be few signs of seeds unless last fall's pods or cones are still on the trees.

B. If you do not intend to follow up on this assignment using tree models, you may want to eliminate step 5.

C. Children will enjoy getting out to observe trees in their neighborhoods. They will find that the most difficult aspects of the assignment are identifying root structures, using clues to make inferences about visitors, and making a tree model.

II. Integration into the Classroom

A. **Tree Observations.** If you are fortunate enough to have trees in your schoolyard or nearby, your class can do their tree observations as a mini-field trip. It will be more fun for students to work in pairs.

B. **Tree Shape Collages.** Have each student choose two different tree shapes (round, weeping, arching, pyramid, narrow column, or broad column) and cut several silhouettes out of brightly colored construction paper. Limit students to two or three colors and encourage them to use nonnatural shades like purple or turquoise. To complete the collages, students should try several overlapping arrangements and glue the final arrangement of silhouettes to a sheet of contrasting paper.

C. **Seed Jars.** Have students bring in jars filled with seeds and pods. You may want to supplement with beans, lentils, corn, and nuts. Combine your resources, putting like seeds together. Then make decorative jars by filling them with layers of seeds and pods. Each layer should be at least one inch wide.

D. **Seed or Leaf Graph.** Use the seeds, pods, and leaves collected by students to make a graph showing how many children studied each kind of tree. Begin by listing on a large chart all the types of trees your students observed. Then have students glue a leaf or seed from their two trees beside the appropriate listing. Children lacking seeds or leaves can substitute a drawing of a leaf.

E. **Leaf Projects.** All these projects use students' leaves.

- Spatter prints or sun prints showing leaf silhouettes.
- Leaf albums with each leaf labeled.
- Leaf outlines filled with interesting colors and designs.

Unit Eight   Arbor Day Tree Study

F. **Drawing Realistic Trees.** Students will be better able to draw realistic trees at the end of their observations than before. Begin by concentrating on branching structure (V- or U-shaped or ladderlike). Encourage students to start at the base of the tree and swing their crayons upward and outward in one free-flowing stroke. Twigs and leaves should partially cover the main branches, and some sky should show through the foliage.

G. **Foliage Designs.** Take your class for a walk to find a tree with "lacy" foliage. As children look up through the tree, have them use crayons to sketch the patterns and designs they see. Then fill in details and textures with fine-tipped marking pens.

H. **Bark-Rubbing Collage.** Ask students to cut part of their bark rubbings into abstract shapes and combine them to make a bark-texture collage.

I. **Circumference Activities.** Have students label each of their circumference strings with a 6-inch strip of masking tape, writing the name of the tree on one side and their own names on the other. Pin the strings on a bulletin board, ordering by length. Look for patterns in size and kind as well as which trees had the largest and smallest circumferences.

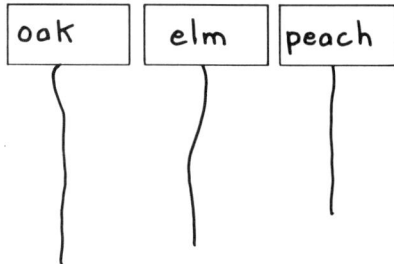

Next ask students to arrange one of their strings in a circle on the floor. How many children can stand inside the circle? Around the circle touching shoulders? How many fit inside and around the largest diameter tree? the smallest?

J. **Vocabulary Building.** Challenge students to list as many of the following as they can.

- The names of all the trees you know.
- All the products you can think of that come from trees.
- All the streets in your town that are named after trees.
- All the words that describe parts of trees and types of trees.

III. Extensions for GATE Students

A. **Tree Census.** Your GATE students will be able to make a tree census of your schoolyard or nearby playground or park. They may need to use a tree identification guide or consult gardening experts to identify less common species. Their census might include the following data.

- Names of trees and number of each species.
- Number of deciduous and evergreen trees.
- Number of trees with U-shaped, V-shaped, or ladderlike branching patterns.

To extend this activity, ask a tree expert to confirm students' identifications and help them label the trees with copper or aluminum markers.

B. **Categorizing Leaf Shapes.** Have GATE students sort the leaves brought in by all the students into these shape categories.

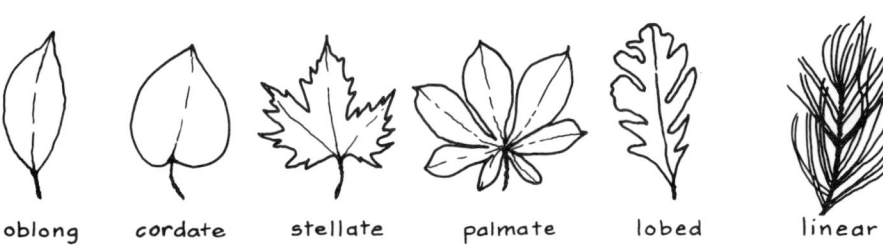

C. **Visitors Learning Center.** GATE students may set up a learning center using a short log or section of a bulletin board. Their job is to create clues of tree visitors for other students to figure out. (Tree visitors might be birds, squirrels, children, etc.) Number the clues and leave paper for recording guesses. Follow up with a class discussion of students' guesses.

D. **Designing a Park.** Ask a group led by GATE students to design a park or playground using the tree models brought in by the class. This activity will work best on a sand table, in a sand pile, or in an area with loose dirt. Before they begin be sure that each child labels his or her model with the tree name and student's name.

The group's first decision will be what kind of park to design. Each kind of park raises different design issues. Here is an example.

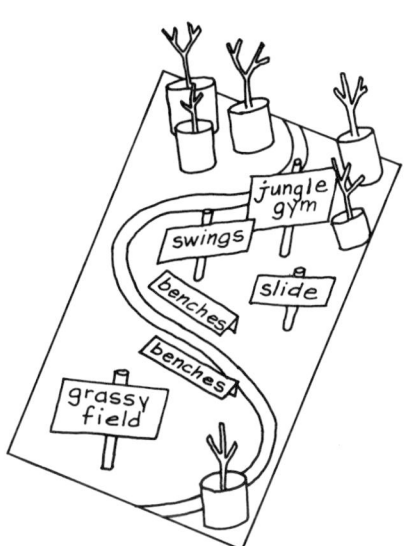

Children's Playground
What kind of play equipment do we need? Where should it go?
Where should grassy areas be placed?
Where should we put benches for grownups to sit and watch?
Where do we want shade? Which trees will provide it best?
How will tree roots affect the playground and grassy areas? Where should the deep- and shallow-rooted trees go?
Where shall we put the trees that are very tall?
Are there some trees that look best planted in groups?
Should we use trees to set the park off from the street?
Do we want good climbing trees in the park? Which ones? Where?
Do we want to encourage animals to live in the playground?
Which trees will attract birds and squirrels?

You will need to help students consider some of the important elements of their park. Or you may wish to enlist the aid of a landscape designer, park planner, or arborist to assist students in their project. Once the general outlines of the park are agreed upon, each student should help lay out paths and play areas and plant the trees. Encourage students to replan and revise as they work. When they are finished, a group spokesperson may describe the park to the class.

E. **Creating a Tree Walk.** Ask your GATE students to map out a walk around the schoolyard with stops at the most interesting trees. This information can be synthesized into a brochure containing a map and descriptions of the special trees. These brochures can be shared with other classes. The creators might also volunteer to serve as docents by giving tree tours.

Name

Date Due

Page 1 of 6

Arbor Day Tree Study

Arbor Day is a day set aside in the spring for planting new trees and enjoying older trees. You will celebrate Arbor Day by studying two trees you enjoy.

Skills you will develop

- observing
- classifying
- measuring
- analyzing—comparing
- synthesizing with a model
- evaluating

What you will need

- pencil
- unlined paper
- tape
- brown crayon
- scissors
- string or yarn
- paper bag
- materials for your model

Before you begin: Read steps 1 through 5. Here is a suggested schedule for this assignment.

Monday: Steps 1 & 2; step 3 for tree 1.

Tuesday: Step 3 for tree 2.

Wednesday: Step 4.

Thursday: Step 5.

Step

Getting Ready to Observe

This week you will observe two trees in your neighborhood. To observe means to watch carefully, to notice things. Make an observation kit with all the things you will need for your tree study. Your kit should include these things.

Unit eight

- paper bag for carrying supplies
- pencil
- brown crayon (peel off the paper wrapper)
- unlined paper
- string or yarn
- tape
- scissors
- observation record (from the next three pages)

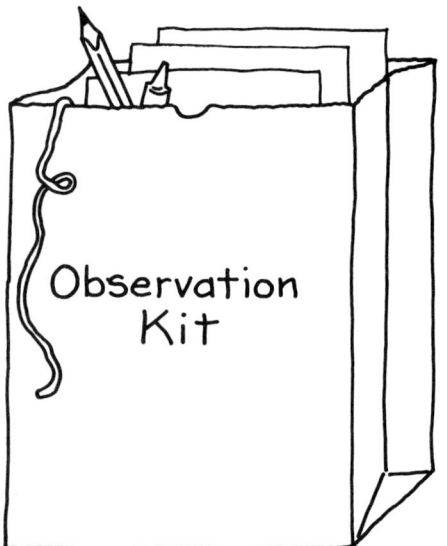

Choosing Two Trees

Take your kit with you as you walk around your neighborhood. Pick out two trees that you would like to study. Be sure they are different kinds of trees. Try to find out the names of both trees and write them here. (Examples: Elm, oak, maple, birch, etc.)

Tree 1_____ Tree 2_____

Observing Your Trees

Take your observation record out of your kit. Do all the activities, A through J, for tree 1. Then do the same activities for tree 2.

Observation Record

A. Tree Shape: Stand back and look at your tree from a distance. This will help you classify its shape. Decide which of these shapes is the basic shape of your tree.

round
arching
narrow column
broad column
pyramid
weeping

B. Is this tree deciduous or evergreen? A deciduous tree loses its leaves in winter. An evergreen tree is covered with leaves or needles all year.

C. Branches: How do the limbs on the tree branch out from the trunk?

U-shaped branches
ladderlike branches
V-shaped branches

Look under the tree for fallen twigs. Put at least five or six twigs in your bag.

	Tree 1	Tree 2
	Name:	Name:
	Draw the shape of tree 1 here.	Draw the shape of tree 2 here.
	Shape:	Shape:
	Check one: deciduous ☐ evergreen ☐	Check one: deciduous ☐ evergreen ☐
	Draw the limbs and branches coming out of the trunk of tree 1. Are they U-shaped, V-shaped, or ladderlike?	Draw the limbs and branches coming out of the trunk of tree 2. Are they U-shaped, V-shaped, or ladderlike?

	Tree 1	Tree 2
D. Roots: Is the tree shallow rooted or deep rooted? Can you feel roots under your feet when you walk barefooted around the trunk? Can you see signs of roots? If not, what does that tell you? Make your best guess. shallow rooted — deep rooted	Check one: shallow rooted ☐ deep rooted ☐	Check one: shallow rooted ☐ deep rooted ☐
E. Seeds: Can you see seedpods, fruits, cones, or nuts on the tree? If you find seeds on the ground, put a handful in your bag. You may have trouble finding evidence of seeds this time of year. When would be the best time to find them?	Draw or tape a seed here if you can find one.	Draw or tape a seed here if you can find one.
F. Leaves and Needles: Look under the tree for fallen needles or leaves. Put several in your bag. If there are none on the ground, draw those you see on the tree. Why isn't it a good idea to pull leaves or needles off the tree?	Draw or tape one group of needles or leaves here.	Draw or tape one group of needles or leaves here.
G. Bark: How would you describe the texture or feel of the bark on the tree trunk? Use descriptive words with *smooth, bumpy, wrinkled,* and *rough.*	Write words that describe the texture of the bark here.	Write words that describe the texture of the bark here.

	Tree 1	Tree 2
H. Bark Rubbing: Make a rubbing of the bark on the tree with your unlined paper and brown crayon. (Use another color if you don't have brown.) Hold the paper against the trunk. Rub the side of the crayon all over the paper. Label the rubbing with the name of the tree.	Cut off a corner of your rubbing and tape it here. Put the rest in your bag.	Cut off a corner of your rubbing and tape it here. Put the rest in your bag.
I. Circumference: Measure the circumference of the trunk (the distance around). Wrap your string or yarn around the trunk. Pull it tight. Use your scissors to cut both ends of the string or yarn where they meet.	Coil the string or yarn and tape it.	Coil the string or yarn and tape it here.

J. Visitors: Be a detective! What clues can you find to tell you who has visited this tree? Use your eyes, nose, ears, and hands in your search for clues.
 	
Possible Clues
  webs
  nests
  holes
  chewed leaves
  carvings
  kite string
  chattering
 	
Possible Visitors
  spiders
  birds
  woodpeckers
  caterpillars
  teenagers
  children
  squirrels
	Clues
	_____
	_____
	_____
	_____
	_____ Visitors
	_____
	_____
	_____
	_____
	_____
		Clues
		_____
		_____
		_____
		_____
		_____ Visitors
		_____
		_____
		_____
		_____
		_____

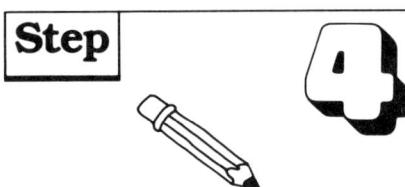

Step 4

Analyzing Your Observations

Look carefully at your observation record to answer these questions. Which of the trees you studied would be the best choice for:

a. a tree house?_____Why?_____

_____

b. a tree planted along the side of a street?_____Why?

_____

c. a tree in a park?_____Why?_____

_____

d. a place that needs shade in the summer?_____Why?

_____

e. a painting?_____Why?_____

_____

f. a forest?_____Why?_____

_____

Step 5

Making a Model of a Tree

Make a model of one of the two trees you studied. You might use a narrow can with a few rocks in the bottom for your trunk. The rocks will keep your model from tipping over. To make the tree look real, use the things you collected in your observation kit bag.

Examples: can + rubbing = trunk
           twigs + leaves = branches

Begin by giving your model the right branch pattern—U-shaped, V-shaped, or ladderlike. Then try to give your model the proper tree shape such as round, pyramid, or arching. You may want to use wire, pipe cleaners, tape, paper, or other materials to help you make your model. How will you use any seeds you collected?

Planning a Festival, Celebration or Fiesta

I. Preassessment Considerations

A. You will be amazed at how easily a party can be planned by children with little effort on your part. The biggest challenge will be for you to believe that it will all come together. This unit has been child tested even with kindergarteners and it works.

B. This assignment requires that the entire class be broken into six committees to plan a classroom celebration. The committees are (1) room decorations, (2) table decorations, (3) refreshments, (4) favors, (5) games, and (6) entertainment. You will need to duplicate a separate page of the committee planning sheets for each committee as well as six copies of planning sheet 2, which is the same for all committees. These sheets are not homework. They should be done at school.

C. The student homework assignment is designed to be used by all committee members to keep track of their responsibilities. The first step may be done in class as part of committee planning.

D. Before meeting with your class to begin this activity, you will need to ascertain how much money is available for refreshments and other supplies. You may also want to line up parent volunteers to help with shopping, food preparation, etc.

E. You should decide in advance how to divide your class into committees. You may want to let students volunteer for the committee of their choice and select their own leaders. Or you can assign students and choose leaders before your first meeting. Either way, committees will run more smoothly if you meet with the leaders and discuss their roles before committees meet.

II. Integration into the Classroom

A. **Class Meeting.** In your initial meeting with the class you may want to discuss the following items.

1. Party theme; this could be a holiday, historical period, literary event such as the Mad Hatter's tea party, or special study topic such as a trip to the moon.
2. Time and day of party.
3. Committee assignments and organization.
4. Allocation of funds among committees.
5. Your expectations for committee operation—role of chairperson, role of members, sharing of responsibilities, etc.

B. **Committee Meetings.** Each committee may need from one to four meetings to complete its plans. At those meetings:

1. Chairpersons should list members' names and phone numbers, read through the planning questions, and record final decisions in the space provided on the committee planning sheets.
2. Members should note any problems or questions they want to discuss with you during their committee appointments.
3. Each student should list his or her committee responsibilities in step 1 of the homework assignments.

C. **Teacher Appointments.** Make an appointment to meet with each committee once it has finished its initial planning. Use this time to listen to the committee's plans and to help resolve any problems. You may need to steer students away from ideas that are too grandiose, complex, or expensive. Encourage students to keep things simple. Before this meeting ends, try to complete the committee schedule in step 4 of the planning sheets. This schedule will help you allocate time for committee work in class.

D. **Follow-up Class Meeting.** After committees have met with you, schedule another class meeting to hear committee reports. This will be a good time to resolve any lingering financial and scheduling problems. Have the class as a whole decide on the sequence of events during the party. (Example: Games, refreshments, entertainment, favors.)

E. **Committee Preparations.** Excitement and a sense of camaraderie will build as committees work together in class to complete their preparations. You may want to invite any adult volunteers working with committees to come into class during this period.

F. **Homework Assignment.** Right around the the time of the celebration, encourage students to complete step 3 (Evaluating your committee).

G. **The Final Setup:** To keep the final setup from becoming a logistical nightmare, try to send most of the class outside while you—or a volunteer—help each committee get ready. You may be able to adapt the following scenario to your classroom.

   1. Room decorations committee: Have this committee put up its decorations during recess or lunch period.
   2. Table decorations committee: Give this group 10 minutes to rearrange tables and desks, set out place settings, and arrange a centerpiece.
   3. Favors committee: If favors are to be put at each place, invite this group in next. If the committee plans to distribute favors during the party, no setup time is needed.
   4. Entertainment committee: Give this group time next to set up a projector, arrange scenery, change into costumes, etc.
   5. Games committee: This group may need a few minutes to set up their games.
   6. Refreshments committee: If possible, have this group finish its preparations in a school kitchen or utility room with the guidance of a volunteer. Otherwise, this should be the last group to make its preparations in the classroom.

H. **Celebration Time.** Relax and enjoy the festivities. The children will take over beautifully.

III. Extensions for GATE Students

You may want to make judicious use of your gifted and talented students when making committee assignments. Gifted leaders can be asked to serve as chairpersons. Children with talents in the performing arts may be most helpful on the entertainment committee. Those gifted in the visual arts might enjoy working on the room decorations, table decorations, or favors committees. Creative students might be best used on the games or refreshments committees.

Name

Date Due
Page 1 of 2

Planning a Festival, Celebration or Fiesta

Nothing is more fun than planning a celebration. This assignment will help you keep track of your planning activities.

Skills you will develop

- organizing a committee
- listening to other people's ideas
- making decisions in a group
- dividing work among committee members
- getting feedback on your plans
- following up on committee jobs
- reporting about your committee work
- evaluating your committee

What you will need

- pencil
- material for your committee work
- cooperative adult

Before you begin: Read steps 1 through 3. Plan to do steps 1 and 2 after you have met with your committee. Do step 3 a day or two before the celebration.

What committee are you a member of? _____

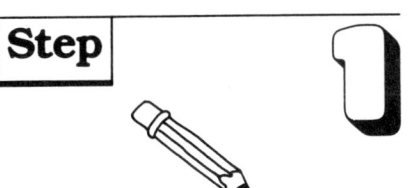

Following Through on Committee Jobs

After meeting with your committee, list the things *you* are supposed to do before the celebration. Check off each job when you have finished it.

Committee Jobs

☐ 1. _____   ☐ 4. _____

☐ 2. _____   ☐ 5. _____

☐ 3. _____   ☐ 6. _____

Now list all the things you need to take to school for the celebration. (Some committee members may not need to bring anything.) Check off each item once you have taken it to class.

Unit Eight

Things to Take to School

☐ 1. _____ ☐ 4. _____

☐ 2. _____ ☐ 5. _____

☐ 3. _____ ☐ 6. _____

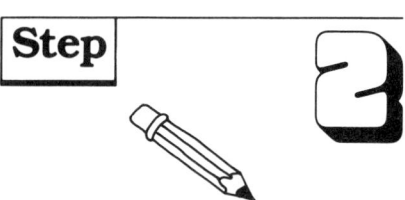

Reporting on Your Committee Work

Make a report to a parent or other grownup about your celebration and your committee work. Talk about your own jobs and the things, if any, that you need to bring from home.

Name of person you made your report to: _____

Evaluating Your Committee

Good committees don't just happen. A committee works well when all its members take part in making decisions and carrying them out. Here are six statements about a good committee. For each one, check whether your committee did well in this area or needed improvement.

1. A good committee knows what its purpose or main job is.
   ☐ did well   ☐ need to improve

2. In a good committee, every member has a chance to present his or her ideas.
   ☐ did well   ☐ need to improve

3. A committee is working well when all members help to carry out the group's decisions.
   ☐ did well   ☐ need to improve

4. In a well-run committee, every member knows what his or her jobs are.
   ☐ did well   ☐ need to improve

5. A good committee finishes its work on time.
   ☐ did well   ☐ need to improve

Tell how you feel about your committee experience.

Name

Date Due

Room Decorations Committee

These committee planning sheets will help your committee do its work. The committee chairperson should read each step to the committee and then write down the members' ideas.

Committee chairperson:

_____

Committee members:

_____

_____

_____

_____

_____

_____

Members' phone numbers in case the chairperson needs to call someone:

( )

( )

( )

( )

( )

( )

Committee Planning

Discuss these questions with the entire committee. Be sure that each member has a chance to share his or her ideas. The chairperson should write ideas on a piece of scratch paper.

Questions for the Room Decorations Committee

1. What kinds of decorations best fit the theme of the celebration?
2. What colors should the decorations be?
3. Can our decorations be made with materials found at school or at home?
4. Where will the decorations be put? On the walls, floor, or ceiling?

Unit Eight

245

Room Decorations Decisions

When the committee decides what it wants to do, write down its decisions here.

Wall Decorations	Ceiling Decorations	Floor Decorations

Halloween Celebration

Name

Date Due

Entertainment Committee

These committee planning sheets will help your committee do its work. The committee chairperson should read each step to the committee and then write down the members' ideas.

Committee chairperson:

_____

Committee members:

_____

_____

_____

_____

_____

_____

Members' phone numbers in case the chairperson needs to call someone:

( )

( )

( )

( )

( )

( )

Frontier Festival

Unit Eight

Committee Planning

Discuss these questions with the entire committee. Be sure that each member has a chance to share his or her ideas. The chairperson should write ideas on a piece of scratch paper.

Questions for the Entertainment Committee

1. What kinds of entertainment best fit the theme of the celebration? (Examples: Songs, a play, skits, a puppet show, records, films, a parade, a contest, a video tape.)
2. What kinds of entertainment would be the most fun to present?
3. Which of our ideas would be easiest to carry out in the time left before the celebration?
4. How long will our entertainment take during the celebration? (If more than 10 minutes, check with your teacher to find out how much time you can have.)

Entertainment Decisions

When the committee decides what it wants to do, write down its decisions here.

What entertainment does the committee plan to present?

_____

_____

How long will this entertainment take during the celebration?

_____

Pet Parade Party

Name _____

Date Due

Games Committee

These committee planning sheets will help your committee do its work. The committee chairperson should read each step to the committee and then write down the members' ideas.

Committee chairperson:
_____

Committee members:

| | Members' phone numbers in case the chairperson needs to call someone: |

_____ ( )

_____ ( )

_____ ( )

_____ ( )

_____ ( )

_____ ( )

Committee Planning

Discuss these questions with the entire committee. Be sure that each member has a chance to share his or her ideas. The chairperson should write ideas on a piece of scratch paper.

Questions for the Games Committee

1. Do we know any games that fit the theme of the celebration? Can we change these games to fit the theme even better?
2. Can we think up new games that fit the theme? How would they be played?
3. Can the games we are thinking about be played by the entire class?
4. Where will we play our games? Outside or inside the classroom?
5. Are the games we are thinking about easy to learn?

6. Of all the games we have discussed, which do we most want to play? Which is our second choice? Our third choice? We will probably have time for only two or three games.

Games Decisions

When the committee decides what it wants to do, write down its decision here.

Game Ranking	Name of the Game	Where It Should Be Played
First choice		
Second choice		
Third choice		

Cinco de Mayo Fiesta

Name

Date Due

Refreshments Committee

These committee planning sheets will help your committee do its work. The committee chairperson should read each step to the committee and then write down the members' ideas.

Committee chairperson:

_____

Committee members:

Members' phone numbers in case the chairperson needs to call someone:

_____ ( )

_____ ( )

_____ ( )

_____ ( )

_____ ( )

_____ ( )

Committee Planning

Discuss these questions with the entire committee. Be sure that each member has a chance to share his or her ideas. The chairperson should write ideas on a piece of scratch paper.

Questions for the Refreshments Committee

1. What kinds of food fit the theme of the celebration?
2. What drink fits the theme?
3. Where can we prepare our refreshments? At school the day of the celebration? At home the day before?
4. Will people need something more than a cup and a plate for their refreshments? (If so, be sure to tell the table decorations committee what they need to provide.)
5. What serving dishes will we need for refreshments?

Refreshments Decisions

When the committee decides what it wants to do, write down its decisions here.

Refreshment	What We Will Serve	Where We Will Prepare It	What We Need to Eat It (cups, plates, spoons)
Food			
Drink			

Outer Space Day Mooncakes and Rocket Pops

Name _____

Date Due
Page 1 of 2

Favors Committee

These committee planning sheets will help your committee do its work. The committee chairperson should read each step to the committee and then write down the members' ideas.

Committee chairperson:
_____

Committee members:

_____ (   )

_____ (   )

_____ (   )

_____ (   )

_____ (   )

_____ (   )

Members' phone numbers in case the chairperson needs to call someone:

Step 1 — Committee Planning

Discuss these questions with the entire committee. Be sure that each member has a chance to share his or her ideas. The chairperson should write ideas on a piece of scratch paper.

Questions for the Favors Committee

1. What kinds of favors fit the theme of the celebration?
2. Which of these favors would be easiest for the committee to make?
3. Which of these favors could be made with materials that can be found at school?
4. Can anyone think of free materials we could bring from home for making favors?
5. What colors should the favors be?
6. How should the favors be given out during the celebration?

Unit Eight

Favors Decisions

When the committee decides what it wants to do, write down its decisions here.

What favors will we make?_____

What colors will they be?_____

How will we give them out during the celebration?_____

_____

Arbor Day "Plant a Tree" Favor

Name

Date Due

Table Decorations Committee

These committee planning sheets will help your committee do its work. The committee chairperson should read each step to the committee and then write down the members' ideas.

Committee chairperson:

_____

Committee members:

_____ ()

_____ ( )

_____ ( )

_____ ( )

_____ ( )

_____ ( )

Members' phone numbers in case the chairperson needs to call someone:

Step 1

Committee Planning

Discuss these questions with the entire committee. Be sure that each member has a chance to share his or her ideas. The chairperson should write ideas on a piece of scratch paper.

Questions for the Table Decorations Committee

1. What decorations should go in the center of the refreshments table? How can we make this centerpiece fit the theme of the celebration?
2. What colors should the table decorations be?
3. What will each person need at his or her place? Plan to provide placemats, plates, cups, and napkins. Check with the refreshment committee to find out if we will need bowls, spoons, knives, or forks.

4. How can we decorate the placemats, cups, and plates to fit the theme?
5. How many place settings will we need?

Table Decorations Decisions

Item	Color	Special Decorations to Fit the Theme	Number Needed
Centerpiece			
Placemats			
Plates			
Cups			
Napkins			
Bowls			
Forks			
Spoons			
Knives			

Hawaiian Luau

Planning Sheet 3 (for all committees)

Step 2 — Deciding What Your Committee Needs

List all the things your committee needs to carry out its plans.

Things Needed	Where Found (Check one)		Who Will Bring This Item to Class
	Home	School	

Step 3 — Dividing the Work

List the things your committee needs to do to get ready for the celebration. Decide which members will do each job. Every member should help.

Committee Jobs	Who Will Do This job

Unit Eight　　　　Planning Sheet (for all committees)　　　　257

Planning Sheet 4 (for all committees)

Step 4: Getting Feedback on Your Plans

Make an appointment with your teacher to talk over your plans. Use this time to bring up any problems or questions your committee has. During this meeting fill out the following schedule with your teacher's help.

Committee Work Schedule

Things to Be Done the Week Before the Celebration	Things to Be Done the Day Before the Celebration	Things to Be Done the Day of the Celebration

STUDY AIDS

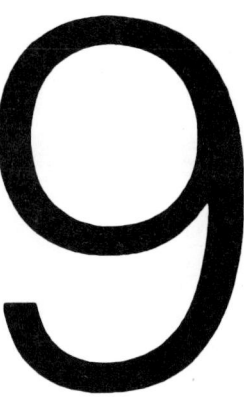

Scope

These eight study aids are designed to be used both in class and as part of homework assignments that you design. They are open-ended and can be used in many curriculum areas throughout the year.

1. Homework Schedule
2. Cluster Diagram
3. Paragraph Planning
4. Individualized Spelling Sheets
5. Spelling Patterns
6. Making a Presentation
7. Writing a Letter
8. Addressing an Envelope

Integration into Your Program

Homework Schedule ■ This schedule can be sent home each week to help students organize and keep track of their homework.

Cluster Diagram ■ Clustering can be used effectively whenever students need to collect and organize information topically.

Paragraph Planning ■ This sheet will help students write well-organized paragraphs on any subject.

Individualized Spelling Sheets ■ Use these sheets with your students' own spelling words to tailor their study methods to their strongest learning modalities and to add variety to your spelling program.

Spelling Patterns ■ See the educator's page for "Detecting Spelling Patterns" in Unit 3 for ideas of other patterns students can explore throughout the year.

Making a Presentation ■ These suggestions may prove helpful whenever students are faced with the challenge of making a report on something they have read, studied, or experienced.

Writing a Letter ■ Whether writing a thank-you note, issuing an invitation, or expressing an opinion, this simple guide will help students put every element of a letter in its proper place.

Addressing an Envelope ■ This companion to "Writing a Letter" will help students get their missives mailed.

Unit Nine

Name _____

Date Due
Page 1 of 1

Homework Schedule

Use this sheet to organize your homework schedule for this week. Begin by reading through your **Mind**Movers assignment quickly. Then decide which steps you want to do each day. If you have other homework this week, divide it over the next few days also.

Keep track of your progress by putting a check in the box beside each item on your schedule when you have finished it.

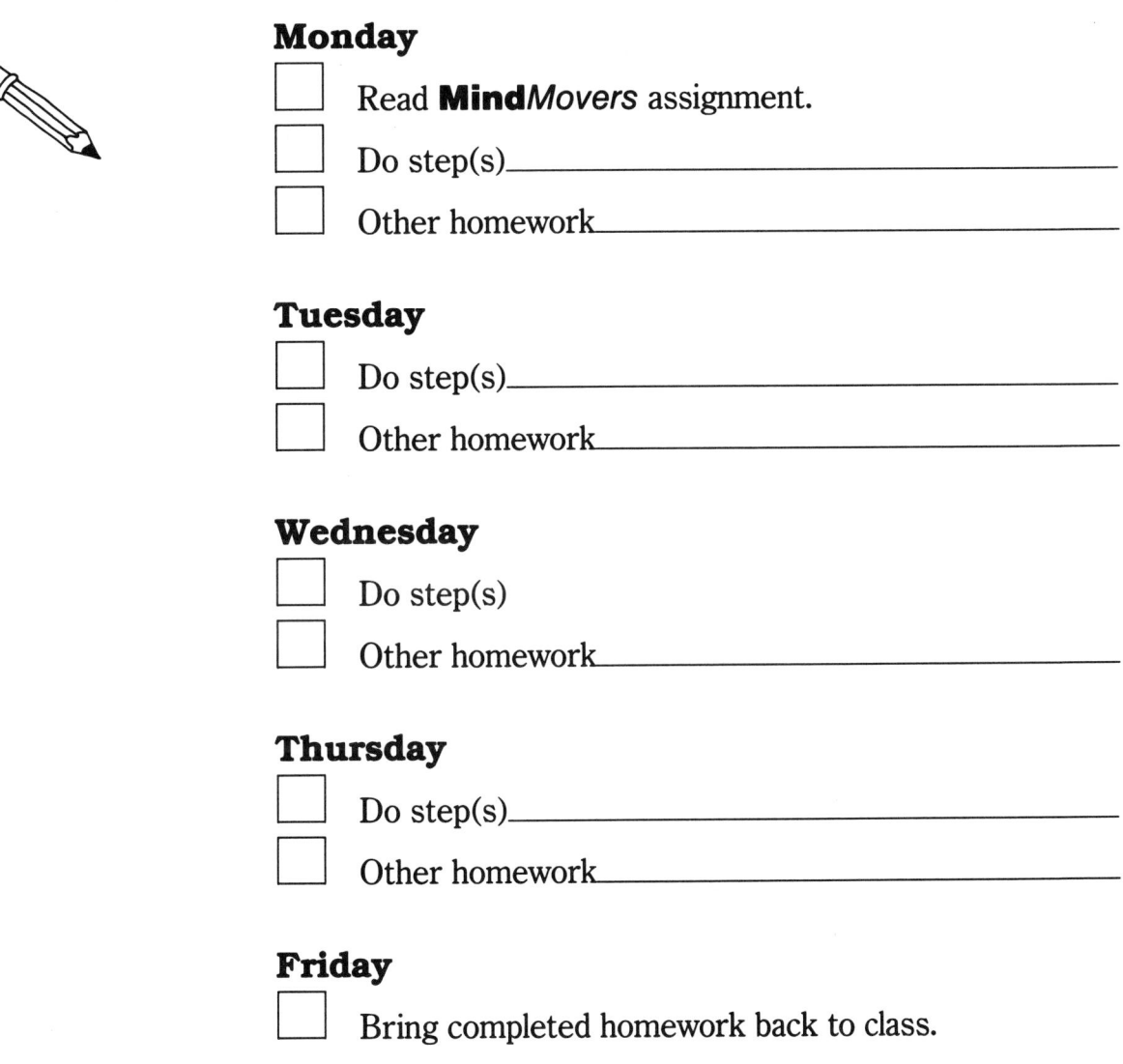

Monday
☐ Read **Mind**Movers assignment.
☐ Do step(s) _____
☐ Other homework _____

Tuesday
☐ Do step(s) _____
☐ Other homework _____

Wednesday
☐ Do step(s)
☐ Other homework _____

Thursday
☐ Do step(s) _____
☐ Other homework _____

Friday
☐ Bring completed homework back to class.

Unit Nine

Name

Date Due
Page 1 of 1

Cluster Diagram

Use this cluster diagram to help you gather and organize information. Write the main topic of your work in the center space. You may want to add other topic circles.

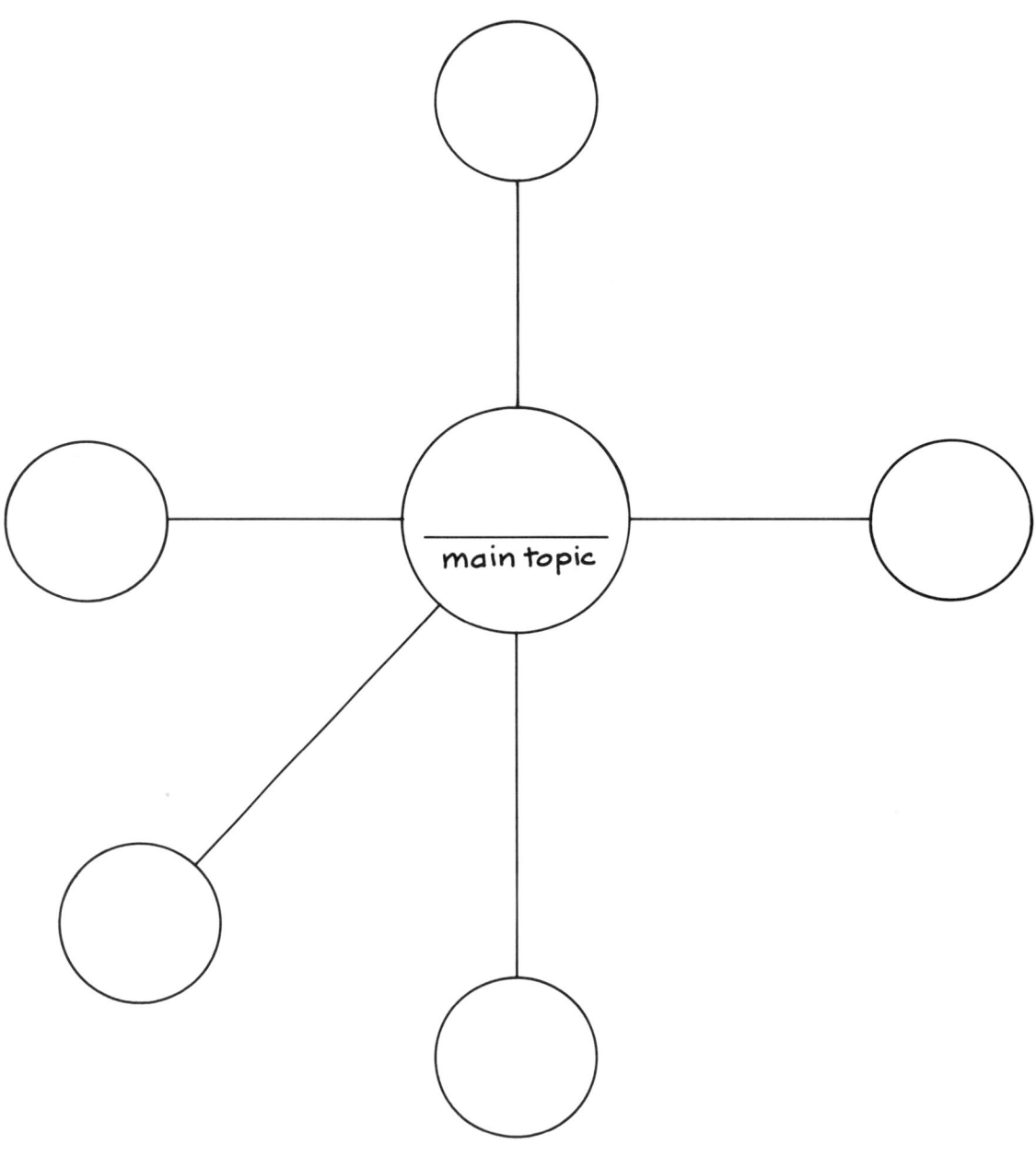

262 Unit Nine

Paragraph Planning

Name _____

Date Due _____

A well-written paragraph has three parts. The first is a topic sentence that tells what the paragraph is about. The second is the information that supports or explains the topic sentence. The last part is a concluding sentence that ties the paragraph together in some way. By planning a paragraph before writing it, a writer is more likely to get all three parts in the right order.

This chart will help you organize a paragraph. As you fill it out, think about the ideas and information you want in your paragraph. You can worry about complete sentences and spelling when you write your final paragraph. Remember, good writing comes from good thinking.

Paragraph Planning Chart

Topic sentence: Tell what the paragraph is about.	Supporting information: List at least two ideas or facts that support or explain your topic sentence. You may list more.	Concluding sentence: Find some way to tie your paragraph together. You may want to say how you feel about the subject. You may tell why it is important. Or you may want to summarize the information in your paragraph.

Unit Nine

Name

Date Due

Individualized Spelling Sheets

See and Spell

Below are five ways to use your eyes and visual memory to study spelling words. Choose one method to learn your spelling words. Write this week's spelling words here.

1. _____   6. _____
2. _____   7. _____
3. _____   8. _____
4. _____   9. _____
5. _____   10. _____

Flashing Lights

Using large letters, write your words on a grocery bag. Take your bag and a flashlight to bed with you. Turn out all the lights. Use your flashlight to light up each word, one letter at a time. Then write each word in light on the ceiling.

Seeing Red

Underline the difficult part of each word on your list. Then write each word in pencil on a piece of paper. Go over the difficult letters in red marking pen or crayon. Example:

S u <u>r</u> p r i s e

Just Your Type

Type out each word on a typewriter, making sure to spell each one correctly. Now type your list a few more times.

Deco-Write

Write out each word using fancy letters. Try several styles of letters for each word.

Art Words

Make a picture that uses each word in an interesting way. Be sure you spell the word correctly.

history

Shoes

Unit Nine

Individualized Spelling Sheets

Name

Date Due

Hear and Spell

Below are five ways to use your ears and auditory memory to learn spelling words. Write this week's spelling words here. Choose one method to learn these words.

1. _____ 6. _____
2. _____ 7. _____
3. _____ 8. _____
4. _____ 9. _____
5. _____ 10. _____

Drum It In
Use your hands or a pencil to create a new rhythm pattern for each word.
Example:

r-H-y-t-H-m

Repeat each word pattern several times.

Cheer Up
Make up a cheer using each spelling word.
Example:
"Poultry, poultry, that's our cry.
P-O-U-L-T-R-Y."
Yell each cheer several times.

Sleep on It
Use a tape recorder to tape yourself spelling each word correctly. Then listen to your tape a few times just before you fall asleep.

Sing It Out
Use a tune you know or make one up to sing as you spell out each word.
Example:
Try singing G-R-O-C-E-R-Y to the tune of "Mary Had a Little Lamb."
Sing each word several times while you take a bath or shower.

Say It Like It Sounds
Say each spelling word aloud as if it were pronounced exactly as it is spelled. Example:

Vegetable—Say it like "vegee-table" to remember that second *e*.

Favorite—Say it like "favor-right" to remember the *o*.

After you say a word the way it sounds, spell it correctly. Do this several times for each word.

Unit Nine

Name

Date Due

Individualized Spelling Sheets

Move and Spell

Below are five ways to use body movement and your kinesthetic memory to learn spelling words. Write this week's spelling words here. Choose one method to learn these words.

1. _____   6. _____
2. _____   7. _____
3. _____   8. _____
4. _____   9. _____
5. _____   10. _____

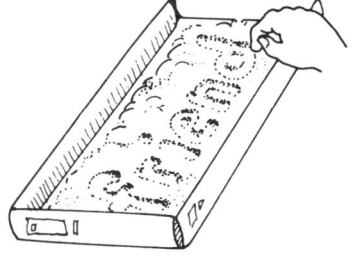

Sweet Talk

Pour one cup of sugar (or salt) into a shoebox lid or shallow pan. Spread the sugar out evenly. With your finger in the sugar, carefully spell out each word.

Water Work

Take a clean paintbrush, a bucket of water, and your spelling words outside. Paint each word in water on the sidewalk, a garage door, or a fence. Make the letters big, and be sure to put them in the correct order.

Back Words

Ask a friend or family member to trace each word on your back with a finger. Guess which word it is. Then spell it back to your friend. Do this until you get all the words right.

Nitty Gritty

Trace each word with your finger on the gritty side of a large sheet of sandpaper. Do this several times for each word.

Leave Your Mark

Find a smooth patch of sand, snow, or dirt. Write out each word in that patch using your hand or a stick. Use your list to spell each word correctly.

Name

Date Due

Spelling Patterns

Step 1: Collecting Words

List as many words as you can that are described here.

_____

_____

(Your teacher will tell you what kinds of words to look for.)

1. _____	11. _____
2. _____	12. _____
3. _____	13. _____
4. _____	14. _____
5. _____	15. _____
6. _____	16. _____
7. _____	17. _____
8. _____	18. _____
9. _____	19. _____
10. _____	20. _____

Step 2: Checking for Correct Spelling

Be sure that all the words on your list are spelled correctly. If you are not certain about any word, look it up in a dictionary. Ask a good speller to go over your corrected list. If any words are spelled wrong, correct them before going on.

 **3**

Analyzing Spelling Patterns

Can you find any patterns in the words on your list? Look them over carefully. Circle combinations of letters that are the same in several words. Say the words aloud and listen for how they sound. Are they alike in some way?

 **4**

Describing Spelling Patterns

Do your best to describe the spelling pattern you have discovered. This may not be easy to do. You may want to ask someone to help you.

_____
_____
_____
_____
_____
_____
_____

Making a Presentation

There are many ways to report to your class on an event, experience, book you have read, or subject you have learned about. You might want to use one of the ideas listed here.

When you have decided how you want to report, think carefully about what you want to present. If you put everything you know into your presentation, it will probably be too big, too long, or too boring. Ask yourself what is most interesting about this subject. What would your class find most interesting? When you have answered these two questions, you will have a better idea about what to include in your presentation.

Presentation Ideas

Poem:
What do you want to write about in your poem?
How will you organize it?
What should the title be?
What will you write your final copy on?
Will you read your poem out loud to your class?

Song:
What do you want to tell about in your song?
Will you use a tune you know or make one up?
Will you need someone else to help you sing your song in class?
Will you need instruments for your presentation?

Flannel board story:
What do you want to tell about in your story?
What scenes do you want to illustrate?
What materials will you need?
Is a flannel board available at school for you to use?
Can you practice with the flannel board before your presentation?
(*Hint:* Paste sandpaper on your pictures to help them stick to the board.)

Picture, poster, or mural:
What do you want to illustrate?
How large should your picture, poster, or mural be?
What materials will you need?
How will you present this artwork to your class?

Display:
What do you want to put in your display?
Where will you set it up in your classroom?
How will you make it interesting and attractive?
What do you want to tell your class about your display?

TV newscast:
What do you want to say in your news report?
Will you illustrate your report in some way?
How should you stand or sit and speak during your report?
(*Hint:* Watch TV news programs for ideas.)

Mobile:
What objects, words, or pictures will you hang on your mobile?
What materials will you need?
Will you need help to make it balance?
Where will you hang it in your classroom?
What do you want to tell your class about the mobile?

Play:
What events do you want to act out?
How many characters will be in your play?
What will each character do and say?
Will you need costumes or props?
Will you perform your play or present it as a written script?
If you perform your play, who will the actors be?

Puppet show:
What events do you want to act out?
What puppets will you need to make or borrow?
What will you use for a puppet stage?
Will you need scenery?
What will your puppets say and do?
Will you need a friend to help you?

Game:
What will the object of the game be?
Will it be a board game, card game, or thinking game?
What will the rules be? (*Hint:* Keep them simple.)
What materials will you need?
What is the name of your game?

Book or comic book:
What do you want to write about in your book?
How will you illustrate your book?
What should the title be?
How will you share your book with the class?

Newspaper story:
What do you want to report about in your story? (*Hint:* Reporters try to tell their readers "Who, what, when, where, and why.")
What will your headline say?
Will you use a picture or illustration with your report?
How will you share your newspaper story with your class?

Model or diorama:
What kind of model or diorama fits your subject?
How large should it be?
What materials will you need?
What will you say to your class about your model or diorama?

Name

Date Due
Page 1 of 1

(Be sure to indent.)

Writing a Letter

Use this form to write a rough draft of your letter. Then copy it carefully onto nice writing paper.

_____
(Today's date)

Dear _____,

_____
_____
_____
_____
_____
_____
_____
_____
_____
_____
_____

_____,
(Closing such as "Your friend")

_____
(Your name)

Check yourself:

- Did I use capital letters to begin names? the month? sentences?
- Did I use commas and periods where needed?
- Is my spelling correct?
- Is my meaning clear?

 **Addressing an Envelope**

Practice addressing an envelope using this form. When everything is correctly filled in, copy the return address and mailing address onto an envelope. Don't forget to put a stamp on your envelope if you plan to mail it.

a. Your first and last name.
b. Your house number and street or post office box number.
c. Your town, state, and ZIP code.
d. Mr., Mrs., Miss, or Ms.
e. Person's first and last name.
f. House number and street or post office box number.
g. Name of town.
h. Name of state. Use the abbreviation if you know it.
i. ZIP Code.
j. Name of country if this letter is going outside the U.S.

Return address

a. _____
b. _____
c. _____

Put stamp here on real envelope.

Mailing address

d. _____ e. _____
f. _____
g. _____, h. _____ i. _____
j. _____

Check yourself:

- Did I spell all the names and places correctly?
- Are the house numbers or post office box numbers correct?
- Did I use the right ZIP codes?
- Did I use capital letters to begin the names of people and places?
- Did I put commas between the names of towns and states?
- Is my writing neat enough for the post office to read?